T0311702

illustrating
Economics

illustrating Economics

Beasts, Ballads and Aphorisms

Kenneth E. Boulding

Richard P. Beilock, editor

Routledge
Taylor & Francis Group

LONDON AND NEW YORK

First published 1980 by Transaction Publishers

Published 2017 by Routledge
2 Park Square, Milton Park, Abingdon, Oxon OX14 4RN
711 Third Avenue, New York, NY 10017, USA

Routledge is an imprint of the Taylor & Francis Group, an informa business

Library of Congress Catalog Number: 2009028399

Library of Congress Cataloging-in-Publication Data

Boulding, Kenneth Ewart, 1910-1993.
  [Beasts, ballads, and Bouldingisms]
  Illustrating economics : beasts, ballads and aphorisms / Kenneth E.
  Boulding ; Richard P. Beilock, editor.
      p. cm.
  Originally published in 1980 under title: Beasts, ballads, and Bouldingisms.
  Includes bibliographical references and index.
  ISBN 978-1-4128-1170-5
    I. Beilock, Richard. II. Title.

PS3503.O756B4 2009
811'.54--dc22
                                                                    2009028399
  ISBN 13: 978-1-4128-1170-5 (pbk)
  ISBN 13: 978-0-87855-339-6 (hbk)

Contents

Acknowledgments

Grateful acknowledgment is made to those publishers granting permission to reprint the following copyrighted material:

Selected lines from "Towards a Pure Theory of Threat Systems," *American Economic Review*, LIII, 2 (May 1963), 434.

"X Cantos," *Michigan Quarterly Review*, VIII, 1 (Winter 1969), 29-31.

Selected lines from *Principles of Economic Policy* (Englewood Cliffs, N.J.: Prentice-Hall, 1958), 1, 110, 159, 285, 313.

Selected lines from "Arden House Poetry," in *Models of Markets*, edited by Alfred R. Oxenfeldt (New York: Columbia University Press, 1963), 369-71.

"Ditchley Park Anthology: Minutes in Verse," *Journal of Money, Credit and Banking*, I, 3 (August 1969), 318, 354, 462, 507, 555, 624, 681. Copyright © 1969 by the Ohio State University Press.

"Brandywine River Anthology," *Michigan Business Review*, 10, 2 (March 1958), 7-9.

"The Feather River Anthology," *Industrial Water Engineering*, 3, 12, (December 1966), 32-33.

"The Old Agricultural Lag," in *No Easy Harvest: The Dilemma of Agriculture in Underdeveloped Countries*, by Max Millikan and David Hapgood (Boston: Massachusetts Institute of Technology Center for International Studies, 1967), xii. Copyright © 1967 by Massachusetts Institute of Technology.

Selected lines from "New Goals for Society?" in *Energy, Economic Growth, and the Environment*, edited by Sam H. Schurr (Baltimore: Johns Hopkins University Press, for Resources for the Future, 1972), 139.

"The Conservationist's Lament; The Technologist's Reply," in *Man's Role in Changing the Face of the Earth*, edited by William

L. Thomas, Jr. (Chicago: University of Chicago Press, for the Wenner-Gren Foundation for Anthropological Research and the National Science Foundation, 1956), 1087.

"A Ballad of Ecological Awareness," in *The Careless Technology,* edited by M. Taghi Farvar and John P. Milton (Garden City, N.Y.: Natural History Press, for the Conservation Foundation and the Center for the Biology of Natural Systems, Washington University, 1972), 3, 157, 371, 669, 793, 955. Reprinted by permission of Doubleday and Company, Inc.

"Isaac Watts Revised" and selected lines from "The Next 200 Years," in *Finite Resources and the Human Future,* edited by Ian G. Barbour (Minneapolis: Augsburg Publishing House, 1976), 160-61, 175.

Introduction

This volume is a selection from the product of well over thirty years of an activity to which it is hard to give a name, which might perhaps be called "significant frivolity." It is an activity which comes out of a state of mind halfway between boredom and total absorption, where the mind floats free in the never-never land of half realistic fantasy. I get into this condition at concerts, at lectures, at conferences, and, above all, in committees. Out of this comes doodles in the shape of drawings or verses or both. I do not take either much responsibility or credit for them. They emerge out of that part of the mind where one stands as spectator. They have given me pleasure; I hope they will give pleasure to others.

The beasts seem to have begun with the "Octoped" drawn on a concert program from Ames, Iowa, in 1945. The originals are on various scraps of paper and leaves from a loose-leaf notebook. I transcribed them onto drawing paper for possible publication in 1959, but the publisher saw fit to refuse them. They lay in my files until, in 1971, my secretary, Vivian Wilson, and Dorothy Carson (then Elise Boulding's secretary) rescued them and published them in a highly limited edition for a few friends. I discovered one beast in the files that did not get into the canon. He is the "Operational Definition," a very practical cat carrying what looks like a hammer and chisel, with a twelve-line verse attached. I promise him for the second edition.

The longer ballads tend to come out of conferences, the shorter ones out of committees. The first that I can recall came out of a two-day meeting on the Impact of the Union (about 1948) at the American University in Washington. John Maurice Clark and I passed quatrains to each other across the table as an offset to the almost uncollectable wisdom of the economics profession. I think one that came out of that occasion was the four-line quatrain:

1

> We all, or nearly all consent
> If wages rise by ten percent
> It puts a choice before the nation
> Of unemployment or inflation

The truth of this remains sadly undimmed by the years. On second thought, I am inclined to credit the first ballad to the meeting of a group working for the Committee for Economic Development (1945) on the transition from war to peace. The transition started very abruptly that August, and we worked almost continuously through the week trying to get out a report. It could well be that the first ballad came out of the coma produced by that experience. The muse continues to strike in this way, though somewhat irregularly. I can never predict if a ballad will emerge from a meeting, though I detect one principle: that if I take colored pencils, the product tends to be art rather than verse.

The "Bouldingisms" consist of a stable of a rather different color. They have been collected from my writings and from recollections of speeches by my old student and friend, Richard Beilock. Without his indefatigable search this volume would never have come into existence. He is responsible, indeed, for editing the entire volume. The "Bouldingisms," of course, come not out of doodling at meetings, but out of "serious" writing. But the state of mind out of which they come is not perhaps radically different from that which produces the beasts and the ballads. Since 1954 I have done most of my writing on the dictaphone, and one gets into a frame of mind here also out of which phrases emerge from the never-never land of the mind, and are, as it were, discovered rather than contrived. I am not sure if all the "Bouldingisms" fall into this category, but perhaps some of them do.

I am most grateful to those who helped to bring this volume to the light of day: Richard Beilock, without whom it would never have come to fruition; Vivian Wilson, my secretary and administrative assistant, whose contribution is so large that her name really should appear on the title page; Janet Heinrichs, my student secretary who typed the manuscript; Irving Louis Horowitz, who took the appalling risk of publishing; and the innumerable people over the years who have produced the states of mind out of which these offerings have emerged.

Kenneth E. Boulding
Boulder, Colorado

Memoirs of a
Pre-Beatle-Liverpudlian
American

I was born on January 18, 1910 at 4 Seymour Street, off London Road, Liverpool, Lancashire, England, Great Britain, Europe, the world, the solar system, the universe. Writing out my full address like this was a great satisfaction when I was a boy. Seymour Street had a solid row of narrow, four-story houses on both sides, each with a flight of steps leading up to the front door, and what we called an "airy," a rectangular hole in front of the basement window, often with steps leading down to a basement underneath the front door. The streets of the neighborhood spoke of the Napoleonic Wars in the early nineteenth century—St. Vincent Street, Rodney Street, Lord Nelson Street. Close by was dirty Lime Street Station; St. George's Hall, a magnificent classical structure, the center of Liverpudlian splendor; the theaters; and the great Picton Library with its huge circular reading room. The neighborhood was very mixed; we belonged to the English minority in Liverpool, a city largely populated by the Irish and the Welsh.

A mile away was the Pier Head on the river Mersey, a mile-wide estuary not unlike the Hudson, perhaps in my childhood even more filthy. We used to say "the quality of Mersey is not strained." At the Pier Head there were three massive commercial buildings—the Liver Building, with two 300-foot towers each crowned with an enormous Liver bird, the mythological symbol of Liverpool; the Mersey Docks and Harbor Board, with its state-capitol-type dome; and the Cunard Building, a Venetian palace on a large scale. The landing stage was a constant delight to a boy; a floating platform half-a-mile long and connected to the mainland with hinged bridges, down which one ran at breakneck

3

speed when the tide was low, up which one panted when the tide was high. Liverpool was blessed or cursed with a thirty-foot tide.

At one end of the landing stage, important, fussy ferryboats went "across the water" to magical places called Eastham, Rock Ferry, Birkenhead, Seacombe, Egremont, and New Brighton. At the other end of the landing stage were the big liners, towering above the crowds, which went to America and Australia and other far-off places in the existence of which I barely believed. As a boy, I explored the endless fascination of the miles of docks with their lock gates, which opened at high tide to let ships in and out, and then closed, leaving a lake full of ships high above the river at low tide. The old warehouses smelled of palm oil and spices. There were boxes and bales and machines coming and going all over the world. In the row of old warehouses called the Goree were cellars where it was said slaves had been kept—a groan from the inconceivable past.

This was the great age of the electric streetcar known to us only as "trams," more vulgarly as the "lecky." These were two-decker. Some white ones were first class downstairs, with faded blue cushions, a wonderful symbol of the class structure of British society. Most of them were red, and third class both up and down. We always went upstairs—it was more fun and we could not afford the first class. The trams were noisy. They clattered up London Road within a few yards of our front door. They started in the early morning and went until late at night. It was only the dead of night that was quiet. A sign by the driver haunted me with its elegance: "Passengers by having the exact fare ready and tendering copper would greatly assist the conductor in the discharge of his duties." The trams went fanwise to the edge of the city, again to magical places—to Fazakerly, Old Swan, Knotty Ash, Wavertree, Calderstones, Toxteth, and Garston. You could go a very long way for a penny. You could even go out to Sefton Park, where there were trees and grass, though we never did this in winter.

I doubt if there were either a tree or more than a few square feet of grass in a radius of two miles from Seymour Street. We went to the country in the summer, but never in the winter. I was taught in school that the trees turned green in spring. I thought this meant that they got moss on their trunks. But I never felt deprived of nature. The human environment, the pavement and the streets, the trams and the ferrys, were exciting and stimulating, and I had the security of a very loving home. It was a dirty city, a product of the coal age. Often in the winter we could hardly see the other side of the street through the black fog. Buildings were all black, sometimes even festooned with soot. Clothes and curtains got dirty overnight in a constantly losing battle against the dirt. But I took all this for granted.

A Loving Family

My father, William C. Boulding, was a working plumber in business for himself. At the back of the house was the yard, a corrugated iron shed full of pipes, wrenches, and blow torches, and other mysterious and rather frightening apparatus. He had two faithful employees, Billy Fox, who was moody and regarded as a little queer, and Billy Sankey, who was short and cheerful. They and my father always smelled strongly of some kind of grease. My father was a gentle man. I never heard his voice raised in anger. He had had a very hard childhood. His father died soon after he was born; his mother married again, a man known in the family legends as "Pa Hardacre," about whom endless stories were told. He was a bigamist. He drove my father out of the house at the age of twelve to earn his own living on the streets of Liverpool. He constantly mistreated my half-aunts, Ethel and Rosie. He died before I was born, but my mother's accounts of him sounded like something out of Dickens. A great family story was the moment when the second Mrs. Hardacre opened the door to a lady who introduced herself as Mrs. Hardacre, whereupon the second Mrs. Hardacre exclaimed, "Well, if you're Mrs. Hardacre, who am I?" and shut the door with a bang. My mother told me that "Pa" spent most of his later days in bed drinking and reading the laws of bigamy.

My mother, Elizabeth, always known as "Bessie," was also a very gentle soul. She only spanked me once. My maiden aunt Rosie, who was a governess with a mincing "refained" accent but with a very good heart, had brought her employers to tea at our house. I must have been about eight or nine. I put on a big Charlie Chaplin act thinking to entertain them, which was taken very amiss. After they left, my mother took me upstairs and spanked me, crying, "You blew your nose in the serviette. What will they think of us? What will they think of us?" My mother came from Chard, a little town in Somerset, in the west of England. Her father, George Rowe, was a blacksmith. Her mother, Mary, was a little country woman full of stories and wise sayings, worn out when I knew her with the strain of raising three daughters respectably on a miniscule income.

Every summer when I was a little boy we went down to Chard

for a month to stay with them, in a tiny house with no inside plumbing. These were happy times for me. I went for long walks along the country lanes by myself, explored the little town, played with the neighbor's children in the fields, visited various relations, occasionally even went on a bus tour to the seaside at Seaton and Lyme Regis. After "the war" (there was only one war in those days), when I was about nine, they came up to live with us in Liverpool on the top floor of our house, which my father fixed up for them as a little flat. He also fixed up a blacksmith shop in the basement for my grandfather. But the days of the blacksmith were over and it never went very well.

My grandfather was a fine, tall, very erect man, with a fine white beard. I was a little afraid of him, especially as I watched him hammer out the red hot iron on the anvil with the sparks flying all over the shop, and then plunge it hissing into the water tank. Sometimes, though not very often, I blew the bellows for him. He was a Methodist, what they called a "local preacher," that is, a lay preacher. My grandmother would tell how he sometimes walked ten miles on a Sunday to take a service at a remote little chapel, then would walk back and collapse on the floor from exhaustion.

After my mother left school (I presume at the age of fourteen), she went up to London and went "in service," that is, into a rich household as a maid. It was there that she met my father at a little Methodist chapel in Bexley Heath, Kent, where my father had been sent on a job. I have a delightful letter written by my grandfather to my father in response to a request for his daughter's hand, rejoicing in the fact that my father was a Christian, but advising him to wait for three years to be sure it was the Lord's will. They did. My mother told me how my grandmother said, when told that my mother was going to marry a man from Liverpool, "Why, you can't go to Liverpool. That is as close to America as you can get without going out of England." It was only two hundred miles from Chard, but it must have seemed like the end of the earth. My mother and father married in 1901, and moved to Liverpool to a tiny house. My mother told me how the first night my father expressed his thankfulness in prayer, and broke down in tears at finally having achieved a home, never having had one when he was a child. They were very happy together in spite of, or perhaps because of, many hardships.

Going to Liverpool was something like going to America in another way. My mother's two younger sisters soon followed her and married Liverpool men. My aunt Ada was little and lively, with a great sense of humor and extremely intelligent. She married a cousin of my father, Frank Boulding, who was an officer in the merchant marine and therefore away a great deal of the time, a huge bulk of a man who hated the sea and had been forced into it. A younger sister, my Aunt Flossie, was tall and rather shy. She married a cheerful little man, Herbert Dowell, who managed a cooperative grocery store and was an ardent member of the Labor party. Since my father was an enthusiastic Liberal, and my Uncle Frank was a Conservative, politics was avoided in our household.

My uncles, my father, and I delighted to play a game of dominoes called "threes and fives." You only scored if the sum of the pips on the four arms was divisible by three or by five, the score being the dividend, and it took me many years to realize this. This may have introduced me subconsciously, however, to the concept of functions. My aunts and uncles lived a tram ride away, but since our house was in the center of town, the family all tended to congregate there. None of them had any children, so I was an only grandchild as well as an only child. My wife has remarked that when I was a boy I really had three mothers.

With "Auntie Ada" I was particularly close. When her monthly allowance came from the shipping company, she would take me down in the morning to an elegant restaurant named Kardomah Cafe, which seemed like another world to me, where we drank hot chocolate, a fantastically exotic delicacy, and listened to a stringed trio, playing I am sure the "Barcarolle" from the *Tales of Hoffman*. My aunt and uncle went to Australia when I was about seventeen. I typed off a letter to my aunt every week and she replied. She ran a boarding house in a seaside resort called Ulladulla, and had a very hard time during the Depression. They came back to England in 1939 just in time for the bombs. A few years ago I was in Canberra and borrowed a car and drove down to Ulladulla, wandered around and asked everybody who seemed to be over sixty if they had known my aunt and uncle. I found someone who had known them very well and had an extraordinary moment of reliving the past.

Methodist Heritage

We were all Methodists. In a cosmopolitan city this gave us a strong identity. To the average university-type American, indeed to any member of the upper class, Methodism is as unknown as the remote culture in Borneo. There is a huge literature on the

Jews, the Irish, and the Italian Catholics, but practically nothing on the Methodists, despite the fact that they had an enormous impact on all the English-speaking countries. This total lack of interest in a fascinating and important subculture is very surprising. Father, mother, and I went to Brunswick Chapel on Sundays, morning, afternoon, and evening. We walked up London Road, with its clattering trams and traffic and department stores, into Moss Street, through the iron gates, and into a yard paved with old gravestones. Here was the chapel, built about 1820, with a finely proportioned classic portico. Inside was a hush, a semicircular amphitheater of boxed pews covered in red baise facing a high pulpit with a choir loft and a handsome organ behind it, lit by large, clear, arched windows. Delicate fluted columns ringed the flat center of the amphitheater. We sat on red cushions in the family pew. I was told the columns had been put in in the early days because, although the roof was spanned by great beams, the congregation felt nervous with such a wide span. Actually the columns did not hold up anything.

The formal service was rigid: a hymn, a Bible reading, a hymn, a prayer, a hymn, another reading, a hymn, the sermon, the final hymn, and the benediction. The congregation was rather scanty, perhaps 100 to 150 people in a building that could easily seat 1,000. The sermons I do not recall. The fire of early days had died down. There were no shouts of "Hallelujah" or "Amen" from the respectable upper-working-class congregation in its best Sunday clothes. But the hymns I still remember, especially those with Handelian, eighteenth century tunes. To understand Methodism, one must read the hymnal, especially the older ones—"O for Ten Thousand Tongues to Sing my Great Redeemer's Praise":

> Long my imprisoned spirit lay,
> Fast bound in sin and nature's night,
> Thine eye diffused a quickening ray,
> I woke, the dungeon flamed with light,
> My chains fell off, my heart was free,
> I rose, went forth and followed thee.

At the core of Methodism was the discovery of a transcendent joy which illumined with a strange spiritual fire the mean, drab, dirty streets and the hard lives of the British working class. The historical evidence for the belief in transcendence was, of course, the Gospels, a gossipy record by some very ordinary people about some quite extraordinary things that had happened to them, proclaiming the extraordinary news that somebody had actually risen from the dead and had been touched, seen, and heard. There were earlier manifestations, of course, in the Old Testament. The sense that another world from some transcendent dimension beyond the common places of our own space and time might reach in at certain times and places and touch this world with its transforming finger was somehow part of the air I breathed as I grew up.

Once the historical evidence was accepted, of course, psychological evidence began, in the form of transformed lives and the development of a culture that was highly supportive in small emergencies, although it might not respond so well to large ones. This was—and is—a faith which is not fatalistic; it is certainly not an "opiate of the people"; it leads into lively activity, and it is frequently psychologically self-justifying. When adversity is regarded as a temporary chastening, we get out of it much faster than if we regard it either as a fatalistic chance or as a wholly undeserved and unjust accident. My father, I am sure, was "twice born." Coming out of a desperately unhappy childhood and youth, he was converted as a young man in a little Methodist mission and took on the life and identity of a follower of Jesus. My mother was "once born," growing up in the security of the lively and simple faith of her parents, without ever passing through any deep crises.

Early Education

Honesty compels me to state what modesty might wish to play down—that I was a very bright boy, and particularly good at passing examinations. My parents took me out of a rather miserable Church of England school at the top of the street and sent me off to a school about a mile away at Hope Street, originally Unitarian, then called "Undenominational." I must have gone there at about the age of ten. The headmaster, Mr. Lewis, who was a socialist and an agnostic, spent a lot of time with me and another bright boy, Ronald Shaw, who became a very close friend. Mr. Lewis coached us for the scholarship examination that would admit us to the high school. This we both passed, and we entered the Liverpool Collegiate School. I was grateful to Mr. Lewis and admired him, though I confess I was a little worried about his soul, something which I never revealed to him.

When I was about fifteen or sixteen I went for a week to a Methodist summer school, at a place called Swanwick, in Derbyshire. Here I met some of the intellectual leaders of English Methodism, especially a man by the name of T.C. Gregory, who later became a Catholic. From him I learned not only that the Christian church had a great intellectual tradition—and by that time I have to confess that I was an intellectual snob—but he also opened up to me the intensity of its poetic and aesthetic tradition, what today we would no doubt call its "right brain" aspects. With his vivid words he brought me in imagination to the foot of the Cross, and I felt there might be indeed a transcendent agony and glory in the universe beyond ordinary experience.

It was about this time that I passed the matriculation exam and had to choose which of the three "sides" of the sixth form I would go into—classics, modern, or science. Classics I had no taste for, but the choice between the modern side (which would have involved literature, languages, history, and eventually the social sciences) and the science side was difficult. A mathematics master, who was also a Methodist, came to our home and persuaded me to go on the science side, where I studied mathematics, physics, and chemistry almost without interruption for three years, eventually winning a scholarship in chemistry to New College, Oxford. After a year of chemistry at Oxford, I decided this was a mistake, and the college allowed me to keep my scholarship and study politics, philosophy, and economics, which eventually led to my becoming an economist. That early foundation in the natural sciences, however, has always been useful, and by changing horses in midstream this way, I at least defeated the appalling tendency of British education for specialization, even though it was another twenty years before I encountered biology.

Pacifist, Quaker, American

In the meantime, however (no doubt in the right brain), I was in the process of becoming a pacifist, a Quaker, and eventually an American. How I became a pacifist is a puzzle to me. It clearly had something to do with my childhood experiences between 1914 and 1919. When I was two or three my father experienced his most prosperous time, and we moved "across the water" to Wallasey, to a little house with a garden. My mother told me how I went out in the garden, looked at the sky, and said, "'Tars, Mommy, 'tars," never having seen these before in the murk of Liverpool. I remember being in bed with my parents and my mother telling me my father was going to join the army and fight the Kaiser. Fortunately, he had varicose veins and was rejected on medical grounds. The business, however, declined because of the war, and when I was five we had to move back into Liverpool to 4 Seymour Street. My mother told me how I cried, for everything was so noisy and dirty. In 1918, my Uncle Bert, a fastidious little man, came home from the trenches, went up into our bathroom, and threw all his uniform out into the fragment of yard below. I watched my mother go out with a hot iron and kill all the lice. A very handsome young cousin from Australia in a fine uniform turned up. He was killed the next week in France. The Jewish family next door, whose younger son was my own age and a lifelong friend, lost their older son in the war. His mother came over and sobbed on my mother's shoulder and cried, "I shall never see him again." My mother commented after she left, "How sad that she thinks that."

I was nearly nine when the war ended. I remember looking out the window on Armistice Day, in the first "two minutes silence," seeing the Irish "shawl women" kneeling in the street. Nobody in my family was a pacifist. There had been a conscientious objector at the Chapel, but his name was spoken of in rather hushed and embarrassed tones, though my mother had a sneaking sympathy for him. It was not until I was fourteen that I had, I recall most vividly, sitting in the bathroom, a "moment of revelation," in which it seemed to me that war was completely incompatible with the teachings of Jesus on which I had been brought up. I could not see how you could love your enemies and then go and kill them. I arrived at this position quite spontaneously, without the slightest contact with anyone else who held this view.

At this time, of course, I had never heard of the Society of Friends. A little later I got hold of a book by John William Graham called *Conscription and Conscience,* which is an account of the sufferings of the conscientious objectors in Britain in the First World War. This started my interest in Quakerism. There was a Quaker in the Liverpool Collegiate School, a very queer duck whom I did not like very much; but I asked him about Quaker Meeting, and he took me to the meetinghouse, actually not far from where we lived, though on a side street I had never before encountered. I have no recollection of my first Meeting, but a little later I began going regularly, finding in the silence, the simple spoken ministry, and perhaps in the faces of some of the people, something that I had obviously been looking for.

I retained, however, my affection for the Methodists. Indeed, when I joined the Society of Friends at about the age of nineteen, I still retained a formal membership in the Methodist Church. At Oxford I found the Methodists much more congenial than the Quakers, mainly because most of the Quakers had been to private schools and were therefore a step or two ahead of me on the stair of the British class system. After I went to America, however, I lost touch with the Methodists and found my religious identity completely within the Society of Friends. Three things have kept me in the Society of Friends all my life. One is the meeting for worship, with its deep communal silence, with the ministry emerging out of it, as an oasis in a very noisy and talkative world; the second is a commitment to peace and human betterment; and the last, a tolerance which permitted a wide variety of theological opinion and religious experience. I met my wife, Elise, in a Quaker Meeting in Syracuse, New York. We have lived all our lives and raised our five children in places where the Quaker community has meant a great deal to us and given us something like an extended family, indeed almost an instant community everywhere we have gone in the world. This is one of the great benefits of belonging to a small sect. This side of my life is reflected mainly in my poetry. I wrote "The Nayler Sonnets" during the Second World War, expanding each phrase of one of the classic Quaker statements by James Nayler, an early leader of the Society of Friends. My "Sonnets From the Interior Life and Other Autobiographical Verse" is a kind of Quaker journal. These volumes are unknown to the literary world.

I became an American almost by a set of lucky accidents, though I can see in my early life a certain drift or predisposition toward this. During "the war," an American doctor, by the name of Keppel (from Syracuse, New York, of all places), came with the American troops in 1918, attended Brunswick Chapel, and was invited to our home for dinner afterwards. He seemed very impressive to me with his strange accent and outgoing ways. He pointed to the "U.S." on his collar and asked me what it meant. Very proudly, of course, I said, "the United States," whereupon he chuckled and said, "Oh no, it means 'us.' " When I was about fifteen my Sunday School teacher gave me a prize, H.G. Wells' *Outline of History.* This book had a great impact on me, more perhaps than my Sunday School teacher, a pale and earnest young man, might have suspected, for I suddenly realized that the Bible, as well as the English history I was taught in school, was a rather small part of the total human story. H.G. Wells, however, did interest me enormously in the United States, toward which he had a curiously reverential approach.

Commonwealth Fellow in America

I got my B.A. from Oxford in 1931 in the Great Depression. I had a little scholarship so I was able to stay on for a year to do graduate work. I applied for a Commonwealth Fellowship to the United States, and somewhat to my surprise, was awarded one to the University of Chicago. My parents, and indeed my friends, thought about my going to Chicago in much the same way that my grandmother thought of my mother going to Liverpool. The then Prince of Wales was a patron of the Commonwealth Fund, and all the fellows were invited to St. James' Palace to receive the royal blessing. I remember walking what seemed like an interminable distance over to the desk where he was sitting. He smiled and said, "Where are you going?" I said, "Chicago." He giggled and said, "Ha, ha, don't get bumped off." I sailed from Liverpool on the *S.S. Laconia,* my family and friends waving me off with yellow dusters which I could still see far out into the river. It was the last time I saw my father. I received the news of his death almost a year later when I got to the Grand Canyon in the middle of a summer's travel around the United States. On the boat, oddly enough, was Alastair Cooke, also a Commonwealth Fellow, the great interpreter of America to Britain. There was also Professor Schumpeter, the great economist. In the ten days of a slow boat that stopped at Cork, Galway, and Boston, we got quite well acquainted, and I later worked with him at Harvard.

In an age of photography it is hard to be surprised by famous scenes. Sailing into New York harbor was no surprise. The Commonwealth Fund, however, took those of us who were going to Chicago up the Hudson River on the old Day Line to Albany, and that was a surprise. Since my knowledge of American scenery had mainly been derived from Western movies, I imagined that America was rather treeless; so to find all those trees was a real surprise. To find a river more magnificent than the Rhine was still another. I remember waking up from my lower berth and peeking out as the train passed through one of the main streets of Syracuse, as it used to do in those days, and then the following day, as the train ground through Gary, Hammond, and South Chicago, I wondered what on earth I was coming to. I had never seen such a hideous agglomeration of industry in my life, not even in Lancashire. The University of Chicago, however, with the Midway and its rather pleasant nineteenth century Oxonian gothic, was about as noble a landscape as the plains could provide. My fellow Commonwealth Fellow was Robert Shone, later Sir Robert, an important figure in the nationalization, denationalization, and renationalization of the steel industry. He also was from Merseyside, and we became good friends.

I went to see my advisor, who was Jacob Viner, the great international trade theorist. I took with me a thesis I had written at Oxford on international capital movements, of which of course I was very proud. He flipped through it and said with a sniff, "Oxford, no footnotes." I discovered to my dismay that I was expected to take courses, almost as if I were back in high school. Viner wanted me to take his famous 301, so I inquired what was in it and said, "Oh, I have done all that and I don't want to do it again," which annoyed him very much. I ended up working mainly with Henry Schultz, the pioneer econometrician, a man of great sensitivity and wisdom. His tragic early death in an automobile accident was a great loss to the profession.

I also worked with Frank Knight, from whom I learned a good deal. I had published a little note in *The Economic Journal,* my first publication when I was at Oxford. I was very proud of this and sent a reprint to Knight, to which he replied, "Professor Knight thanks Mr. Boulding for his reprint, which he thinks is as confused and wrong as it is possible to be." This got our relationship off to a good start. As a matter of fact, he was probably right about the article. His courses were highly disorganized but very exciting, with new ideas shooting off his head like a Catharine wheel. I always felt that he had an enormous engine of a mind, but practically no clutch to move his ideas forward. But he was immensely stimulating.

In the next room in the gothic quadrangle where we lived, Burton Court, was Albert Hart, a graduate student in economics from New York State, who had an immense flow of rapid-fire, alarmingly coherent conversation, and again threw off ideas at an enormous rate. I have stolen some of my best ideas from him, and again we became very close friends. Chicago was an enormous improvement on Oxford, for which I still have an intense love-hate relationship. With my Liverpool accent, speech impediment, and Methodist teetotalism, I was definitely not accepted at Oxford. I had applied for a fellowship at Christchurch, and with the usual Oxford incompetence they returned to me all the confidential letters that had been written on my behalf by my tutors, all of which said in effect, "This is a bright boy, but he is not one of us." At Chicago nobody asked if I was one of "them"; I was accepted immediately and fell into a circle of very good friends. My first week at Oxford in 1928 (I had gone up a week early to take some examinations) six of us dined together in the vast hall of New College. For a whole week nobody spoke to each other because they had never been introduced. Even though I gradually made a circle of friends at Oxford, mainly from among the outcasts, I never felt either accepted or at home. The friendliness, acceptance, and intense intellectual life at Chicago was a revelation. This was in the early days of President Hutchins. The campus was buzzing with ideas. After six months a whole gang of us moved into the new International House on the Midway.

In the summer of 1933 Robert Shone and I and a friend of ours from New York, a linguist, Bob Hall, went off on our summer travel with a tent in Bob Hall's magnificent open Buick. We went to Minneapolis, crossed the Dust Bowl on washboard dirt roads to Salt Lake, the Tetons, Yellowstone, Glacier, the Canadian Rockies, Seattle, San Francisco, Los Angeles, the Grand Canyon, reveling in the vastness and variety and sheer energy of the continent, in spite of the fact that this was the depth of the Great Depression. At the Grand Canyon I got a cable saying my father had died. I went straight back to England to settle up his affairs. He had kept most of his accounts in his head; he was bankrupt. After ten days of trying to straighten out his accounts, I learned more economics than any other ten days in my life. He was a man of solid goodness and would have been a wonderful teacher. Life forced him into an uncongenial occupation. He was a victim of his times and the Great Depression.

That fall I went back to Harvard to study with Schumpeter, but after a few weeks came down with a rare disease, a spontaneous pneumothorax, and had to spend some eight weeks recovering in the old Stillman Infirmary. My mother sold up in Liverpool and joined me in December before I was out of the hospital. The people in Cambridge were incredibly kind to her. Professor Taussig, whose class I was sitting in on (it was the year he retired), a great gentleman, personally found my mother a place to stay and paid for it out of his own pocket. What an incredible country! When I recovered we went out to Chicago and spent the next six months there. I had given up courses or any thought of a degree, and

ended up working on my own, mainly in capital theory, and published two or three articles as a result.

Teaching at Edinburgh

That June I wrote a play, fell in love, and was rejected—it turns
out rather fortunately. My mother and I went back to Liverpool. It
was the depths of the depression. We had no home; she lived with
her sister, I with a cousin. Our resources dwindled rapidly. There
were only two jobs going in England in economics that summer. I
was turned down for one. Just as we were about at the end of our
resources I got the other at Edinburgh, as a very humble assistant
and two hundred fifty pounds a year. What a relief! We bought a
little apartment in a duplex overlooking the Firth of Forth. After
the comforts of central-heated America, it was cold. In the winter
we would have breakfast with our feet in the gas oven in the kit-
chen, trying to warm up a little bit while the coal fire in the living
room took the edge off the chill.

Intellectually, also, after Chicago, Edinburgh was bleak. The
professor was Alexander Gray, who had written earlier what is
still an excellent book on the classical economics. However, he
had lost interest in economics, and since it was his predessor who
had appointed me, he did not think much of a brash young Eng-
lishman, fresh from Chicago. Twenty years later he wrote me a
charming letter, saying, "I seem to have been mistaken about
you!" The senior lecturer was a charming Scottish lady who was
very kind to me, but who thought everything that had happened
since 1914 was a regrettable interregnum which would soon pass
away. It is hardly an exaggeration to say that the intellectual life
in the department was nil. I passed Adam Smith's grave every
day as I toiled up the Canongate on a bicycle, usually against the
wind. The students seemed unresponsive. About the only bright
spot was the relatively new Friends Meeting, where I made some
good friends. I was working on a big book in economic theory
which never came to anything.

In the second year at Edinburgh I got involved in a study of
British agriculture headed by Lord Astor, which helped out considerably with my income and got me interested in the practical
aspects of economic policy. In the course of this study I spent a
weekend at Clivedon, the Astors' famous home on the Thames. To
me it was almost like being entertained at Versailles by Louis

XIV. I learned a lot in the course of this study about milk-marketing boards, the utter folly of government price policies, and the importance of the age distribution of cows.

Colgate University

In 1937 the Society of Friends had a world conference in Philadelphia at Swarthmore College and I was sent as a delegate from Scotland, with my fare paid. While at the conference I had a phone call from a friend I had known in Chicago telling me there was a teaching job going at something called Colgate University in upstate New York. After the conference I went up on a sleeper on the old Delaware, Lackawanna, and Western (the "Delay, Linger, and Wait," as we called it) to Binghamton. Shaving in the men's room as we were approaching Binghamton, I got in a conversation with a gentleman who lived there, who promptly invited me out to his house for breakfast, since I had some hours to wait for the train up the Chenango Valley. His wife was a little dismayed at the sudden arrival of an unexpected guest. I shall never forget the sense of astonishment at the totally unexpected things that could happen to one in this extraordinary country. I never saw him again and I am not sure that I ever knew his name, but such an act of spontaneous friendliness to a stranger had something to do with the decision that led to my becoming an American.

I got the little train up the valley, spent a day or two in the idyllic village of Hamilton, looking it over and being looked over. With the college on the hill and the Greek revival houses around the triangular green, it was a charming place and still is. I must have made a reasonably good impression, for they offered me an instructorship at $2,000 a year. Since I was supporting my mother I did not think I could live on that, so I turned them down and started down the Hudson to the boat to go back to Britain. By some miracle the department chairman, "Tige" (for Tiger!) Shortliffe, got hold of me by phone in Poughkeepsie and offered me a $400 raise. I was so touched by this that I accepted it. Instead of going down the Hudson to New York and back to Britain, I went up the Hudson to Utica, got a dilapidated jitney over to Hamilton, and eventually became an American. On such a thread does one's life sometimes hang.

The next year my mother sold up in Edinburgh and came over

and joined me. She lived in Hamilton almost the rest of her life and was very happy there. I look back on Hamilton, indeed, as a kind of utopia of gentle, kindly people, who accepted us immediately for what we were, never asked who our grandfather was, and took us immediately into their homes and their societies. I cannot now remember anybody in the four years that I was there who was really mean. Perhaps the mists of time have gilded the scene a bit. The instructorship was hard work, with very heavy teaching loads. The Economics Department had nine people, in a college of a thousand. We used almost every educational device known to man—tutorials, seminars, small classes, and by present-day standards, a fantastic faculty/student ratio. The students were fair, and they worked hard for the most part. Football, of course, was a big thing; but it did not bother anybody that I never understood it. In the department there was a lot of discussion and intellectual life. Keynes's *General Theory* had recently appeared, the Great Depression was still on, the New Deal was thrashing around; it was a good time for employed economists.

The president, a "bluenose" Baptist from Nova Scotia, the nearest thing to an ogre in that paradise, is reported to have said, "I waited 'til the Depression and got a good faculty cheap," which he certainly did. He did not believe very much in democracy or faculty meetings, but he united the faculty against him, got the institution through the Depression, and in the end was respected even if not loved. The hills around were beautiful. I walked over them a great deal. I shared a car with a friend on the faculty. Our friendship survived it, even the fact that I had to go with him on his honeymoon. It was at Colgate that I wrote *Economic Analysis* in two summers. I sent the manuscript off to Harpers, quite blindly, and had it immediately accepted. This in a sense served me as a substitute for the Ph.D. which I never took or wanted to take.

I was active in the Society of Friends in upstate New York. We had a little meeting that met around in various towns in the Mohawk Valley. Then came the war, in which it was hard to be a pacifist. But on that issue I burned my boats behind me. The emotional strain of the times, however, especially the contrast between my idyllic surroundings and what I knew was happening to my friends in Europe, expressed itself in verse, and I began the Nayler Sonnets. In May 1941 at a Friends Quarterly Meeting in Syracuse I found myself sitting almost knee to knee with a disturbing presence. Her name was Elise Bjorn-Hansen. She was

Norwegian by origin, just about to join the Society of Friends. We were engaged in eighteen days and married in two months. We started our married life in Princeton, where I had a job with the old League of Nations Economic and Financial Section. From there we went to Fisk University at Nashville, to Ames, Ann Arbor, and finally to Boulder. We produced five children. We have both written a lot of books, have been president of this and that, and have had a marvelously good life.

These years of maturity will have to be passed over very briefly. The year at Fisk was a good year, though we were never invited into a white home off the campus. I could not resist, however, the invitation to become a labor economist at Iowa State College, which came from Theodore Schultz. I did not really become a labor economist, though I spent a year trying to become one. This did lead, however, to the loss of my purity as an economist, with the development of my interest in general social science and eventually general systems. Iowa State College at that time was a remarkable institution. It had the spirit of a great university, a first-rate faculty, and its feet in the soil and in the needs of the people of the state. Here was liberal education developing not as a leftover from the Middle Ages, but as a response to the needs of the modern world.

In the middle of the Ames years we went up to McGill in Montreal for a year and almost became Canadians. If we could have found a place to live in Montreal at that time, we might have done so; but much as we liked both McGill and Montreal, the call of a larger society was too great and we went back to Ames. After Ames there were eighteen very fruitful years at the University of Michigan in Ann Arbor. Here I had a seminar in the Integration of the Social Sciences, which led eventually into general systems. A year spent at the Center for Advanced Study in the Behavioral Sciences at Stanford, 1954-55, its first year of operation, was a seminal year that gave rise to much of what I did in the following period. Out of this came not only the Society for General Systems Research, of which I was a founding father, but also the *Journal of Conflict Resolution* and the Center for Research on Conflict Resolution at the University of Michigan (now, alas, only a memory), of which also I was a founding father. This was part of my involvement in the larger movement for peace research, in which Elise also participated very actively.

In Ann Arbor we found a very vigorous and stimulating community, not only in the university, which was first-rate and a much more lively environment than the Eastern Seaboard institutions, but also in the very active Friends Meeting, which provided us with an extended family for ourselves and our children. As the children grew older, Elise was able to finish her Ph.D. in sociology.

The move to Boulder in 1967 was inspired partly by the better opportunity there for Elise to follow her career; partly by better conditions of work for myself, with a half-time teaching and a half-time research appointment and a full-time secretary, Vivian Wilson, who has enormously increased my productivity in these years; and of course also by the agreeable physical environment and climate. Again, we found a lively university community and an active Friends Meeting, and a setting for a renewed burst of activity which we are still enjoying.

Becoming An American Citizen

It remains to tell the story of how I became an American citizen. It was in a big courtroom in Des Moines, Iowa, in December 1948. My citizenship application was being opposed by the Department of Naturalization because of my unwillingness to promise to bear arms. After the ordinary cases had been cleared away, my two excellent lawyers got me into the witness box and questioned me for almost an hour. We thought we would almost certainly have to appeal this to a higher court. The judge had been notoriously unfriendly to conscientious objectors all through the war, having sent them all up for five years in prison almost without exception. He sat up on the dais looking like a stone through all of this. At the end of my testimony he turned to me and said, "Do you believe in law, Mr. Boulding?" I said, "Yes." And he said, "Do you believe that the judge should be influenced only by the evidence presented in the court?" I said, "Yes, I think that is a sound principle of Anglo-Saxon law." Then he said, "Why did you ask my cousin [who was a colleague of mine] to intervene with me on your behalf?" I said, "I did not." The friend who had written to his cousin was in the courtroom, along with a good many other friends. He rose and told the judge that he had done it, whereupon the judge called him down to the bar and gave him the tongue-lashing that he was reserving for me for interfering with the majesty of the law. Then, a bit taken aback, he said "Strike that from the record," gave his opinion that he did not approve of the state of the law, but that my lawyers had demonstrated according to the cases cited that I was entitled to citizenship, and he therefore admitted me. There was a bit of confusion about affirming instead of swearing, and I was in. The Department of Naturalization appealed this decision, but for some reason I never discovered, the appeal was withdrawn in Washington. It was courageous of the United States to let me in, and I got a remarkable sense of what it meant to have a government of laws and not of men.

My admiration for the Constitution, still more for the political culture of the United States which sustains it, remains very high. I have felt myself extremely free to criticize my government. I helped to start the first teach-in at Ann Arbor, which I sometimes feel started the avalanche that swept President Johnson and eventually the Vietnam War into the backrooms of history. I ask myself, "What have I contributed to American life?" I find the question hard to answer. Perhaps my most important contribution is half the genes of our five children, spread now from coast to coast, all of them extraordinarily different, but each making a quite noticeable contribution to the ongoing life and the gene pool of society. In my verse I think I have only rarely struck the universal resonances of real poetry, though I flatter myself that it is competent in form and significant as a record of experience. It is despised by the poets, but continues to find a niche in the minds of readers who respond to what may be the peculiar set of experiences that it describes.

Intellectual Contributions

In economics and in my other scientific work I have received abundant recognition, more than anyone could reasonably want. But I do have the uneasy feeling that nobody has really listened very hard to what I had to say. I have made two significant contributions to economic thought. The first was in my *Reconstruction of Economics* in 1949, in which I reconstructed economics, or at least rearranged it, around the concept of stocks of economic goods rather than flows as the primary reality, with an essentially ecological theory of the production (births) and consumption (deaths), and therefore the growth and decline, of the populations of these various species of economic goods. In this volume also I developed a theory of profits based on accounting identities, developing the "widow's cruse" theory of Keynes, as he suggested in his *Treatise on Money*. I regard the distribution of national income between profits, interest, and labor income as determined dynamically by the whole complex of decisions involving dividend distributions, investment, and borrowing, and not determined except indirectly by wage bargains. This view has never passed into the mainstream of economic thought, though it continues to exist in a kind of underworld. It is the key to the understanding of the stability and the eventual fate of capitalism. There are some flaws in the *Reconstruction,* and I never followed it up with the empirical work which might have convinced people of the truth of the theory.

My second contribution to economics is the development of the theory of the grants economy, that is, the economics of one-way transfers. By a happy accident this enterprise has become much better organized than my other work. I became interested in grants mainly out of my interest in the problems of conflict, particularly in the question as to why some conflicts were fruitful and some were not. The main reasons lay in the integrative structures of society, such as those which involve the sense of community and of shared identity. As an economist I naturally thought of the measuring rod of money and the use of the grant (that is, the one-way transfer of economic goods) as a measure of integrative structure, on the grounds that if I give somebody $100 and they just give me a nice smile, this suggests there is some kind of integrative relationship between us. I got a small grant from the Ford Foundation to study "grants," and with this took on a young man from Michigan State University, Martin Pfaff. He turned out to be an extraordinary entrepreneur, who perceived not only the importance of the idea but was able to organize it into an Association for the Study of the Grants Economy, into symposia, papers, proceedings, and together with Professor Janos Horvath at Butler University, created what might also be called a movement. This, however, is still regarded with great suspicion by the mainstream economists, who are so wedded to exchange that they find it hard to take the one-way transfer seriously.

I have made contributions to peace research and international systems. My book *Conflict and Defense* is really an attempt to apply economics, particularly oligopoly theory with a dash of general systems, to international systems. Elise and I helped to organize the Consortium on Peace Research, Education, and Development in 1970, and I have been quite deeply involved in the International Studies Association. I was at the University of Texas as the Tom Slick Distinguished Visiting Professor of World Peace in the Lyndon B. Johnson School, where I gave a seminar on peace research and also some lectures on policy for peace, which became a book, *Stable Peace* (University of Texas Press, 1978). In the last twenty years in the peace research movement my right-brain pacifism has interacted very strongly with my left-brain social science to produce what I hope will be a contribution to a nonutopian and pragmatic movement toward stable peace. However small this contribution, it may be my most important one, for both the United States and the human race are more threatened at the moment by the danger of escalating armaments and nuclear war than they are by anything else.

I have really had an almost indecently good life, much better than I deserve, and it would not have been nearly as good if I had not become an American. A few years back I read avidly the novels of C.P. Snow, feeling a curious affinity for his hero, who also was a bright boy out of the British working class, who stayed in England. I kept feeling I was reading about the life I might have lived if I had not become an American. It was certainly not bad, but it did not have a certain sense of largeness and a sheer human warmth that my life in America has given me, and for this I am deeply grateful, even though my primary allegiance is to this lovely blue and white planet and to the extraordinary experiment that is going on here.

The Unbelievable Success

The Unbelievable Success
Is fostered by the World's caress,
But usually comes to grief
In trying to confirm belief.

The Moon-Faced Barp

The discontented Moon-Faced Barp
Is not particularly sharp —
He calls the Universe in question,
For what is mostly indigestion.

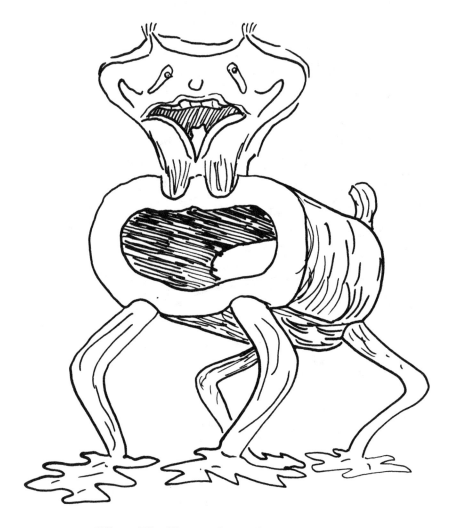

The Hollow Mockery

How happy is the Hollow Mockery,
Because he thinks he's made of crockery!
For from this theory it would follow
That it is virtuous to be hollow.

The Cross-Eyed Scrub

I would not recommend the Scrub
To any decent Woman's Club,
Though kind his heart and good his mind,
His manners are quite unrefined.

Human Nature

The man who goes into the world believing that everyone is his enemy will very soon find his suspicions confirmed.
The Image, 1956, p. 125.

We all tend to value highly what is scarce in our own particular part of the field . . . the sick make a religion of health; the violent make a religion of love; and the self-centered make a religion of objectivity.
The Image, 1956, p. 51.

We are so hypnotized by the power of positive thinking and the supposed necessity to be active that we underestimate the enormous power of taboo and passivity. One recalls an apocryphal story that Eisenhower once said to Dulles, "Don't just do something, stand there."
Stable Peace, 1978, p. 108.

One of the things that is a little puzzling in the human process is why, when benevolence is so clearly beneficial to all (I help you, you help me, and we all go up together) and malevolence is so clearly injurious to all (I beat you down, you beat me down), malevolence is so absurdly popular and easy to learn.
"The Meaning of Human Betterment," 1971, p. 5.

> Four things that give mankind a shove
> Are threats, exchange, persuasion, love;
> But taken in the wrong proportions
> These give us cultural abortions.
> For threats bring manifold abuses

> In games where everybody loses;
> Exchange enriches every nation
> But leads to dangerous alienation;
> Persuaders organize their brothers
> But fool themselves as well as others;
> And love, with longer pull than hate,
> Is slow indeed to propagate.
> "Towards a Pure Theory of Threat Systems," 1963, p. 434.

All too often negative-negative thinking masquerades as positive, especially among the radicals, who think it is sufficient to be against evil rather than for good.
"The Power of Negative Thinking," 1978, p. 55.

The besetting sin of most clever people is that it is much easier to say clever things than true ones.
"Minus the Spark," review of John Kenneth Galbraith, *Economics and the Public Purpose,* 1974, p. 81.

After sixty years I have come to believe that the creative things happen in the cracks within the system.
Creative Tension, 1974, p. 4.

A lady's expensive hat turns to psychic ashes on her head when she sees another lady wearing the same model.
"Economic Theory: The Reconstruction Reconstructed," 1957, p. 29.

Nag's Law

All good things come by nagging. It is not the flash of brilliance, or even the outburst of creative expression that really changes the world. It is the nagger who really changes things — the man who will not take no for an answer, who keeps at it day in and day out, whose strength is as the strength of ten because his heart is pure, who is importunate like the widow in the parable, who has the vision that cannot be denied and who therefore will not be denied.
"Foreword," in *The People: Growth and Survival,* by Gerhard Hirschfeld, 1973, p. xiii.

The discovery of what we have known is always among the more agreeable mental exercises.
"In the Money," Review of Ferdinand Lundberg, *The Rich and the Super-Rich,* and Ben B. Seligman, *Permanent Poverty: An American Syndrome,* 1968, p. 40.

We have state lotteries . . . and the fact that we have no moral objections to this kind of thing now suggests that the popular demand for equality is largely a fraud.

"Justifications for Inequality: The Contributions of Economic Theory," 1975, p. 13.

Anything that we have made sacrifices for we feel almost compelled to identify with; otherwise the sacrifices would have been in vain. . . . At the lower end of the moral scale, this is the fool persisting in his folly, because to admit that it is folly would be to admit that he is a fool, and this he cannot do. . . . At the upper end of the moral scale, this is the martyr going cheerfully to death for his faith, the soldier dying for his country, the mother sacrificing for her child.

"The Role of Legitimacy in the Dynamics of Society," 1969, p. 5.

A people that thinks it knows where it is going, and has a clear idea of its future, has an advantage over one that does not, even though its image may be false and its prophets deceivers.

"Organizing Growth," 1959, p. 36.

The human mind is a vast ballroom. Most of us can paint ourselves into a tiny corner of it because we learn not to learn.

Ecodynamics, 1978, p. 123.

It is hard to reduce an insult to mathematical form, for the reduction has to be so great.

Conflict and Defense, 1962, p. 97.

When the golden egg gets big enough, the temptation to kill the goose seems to be almost irresistible.

"Evolution and Revolution in the Developmental Process," 1967, p. 23.

Excuses are always more important than reasons . . . even the flimsiest of excuses can produce results which the best of reasons cannot supply.

"Space, Technology, and Society: From Puff-Puff to Whoosh," review of Bruce Mazlish, ed., *The Railroad and the Space Program: An Exploration in Historical Analogy,* 1966. p. 979.

Being in the peace-and-good-will-to-all-men business isn't easy, and I can't help noticing that a lot of misery is self-inflicted, and that a lot of rich people are miserable.

"Yes, Virginia, There Will Be a Year 2000," 1977, p. 2.

It would be hard to build an ideology around the multiplication table, for nobody would be against it.

The Meaning of the Twentieth Century, 1964, p. 164.

The infusion of a sense of righteousness into the common urge to bash things around has always proved to be a powerful stimulus to action.

The Organizational Revolution, 1953, p. 162.

Night Thoughts from My Own Couch

I am not greatly overjoyed
In contemplating Sigmund Freud,
Nor do I count myself among
The ardent followers of Jung,
And yet like every normal lad
I hate my Mother and my Dad.
(A natural feeling which extends
To sisters, cousins, aunts and friends.)
I do not know exactly how Ma
Gave me all my little trauma
Or in what manner Papa's sex is
Linked to all my guilt complexes.
But Ma (and I) would have done better
If no Papa had ever met her.
For parents are the only source
Of most neuroses now in force.
And parents, being dull or lazy
Tend to drive their children crazy.
And so my deep subconscious wish
Is this: to have been born a fish.
For fish do not have either sex
Of parents breathing down their necks
And live their unrestricted lives
Devoid of husbands or of wives.
Their mental difficulties browse
On thoughts of food instead of fraus
Their price for straying off the beaten
Path is simply — being eaten!
An end as quick and neat and useful
As man's is slipshod and excuseful.
The evolutionary plan
May not in fact be aimed at man
Who may be climbing on a slim
And quickly tapering branch or limb
While the main trunk prepares a race
Of super-fish to take his place
Who will not need to ease their grouches
On psychiatric couches
And so will move thru future oceans
With perfectly adjusted motions.

*

But contemplating these perfections
Sets off the thought in new directions,
Total perfection well may be
Perfect insipidity
And fish, even at point of nesting
Are not extremely interesting
And so on second thoughts I'd rather
Stick to Mother and to Father.
And be content with being human
Like Harry S. and Mrs. Truman.

Unpublished, 1960.

The Psychoanalytic System

The Psychoanalytic System
Remembers who, how, where, what kissed him
In mingled streams of joy and guilt
And on these blocks his life is built.

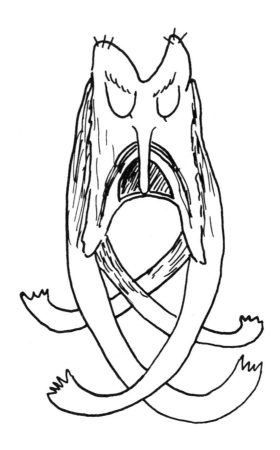

The Unventilated Dripp

The Poor Unventilated Dripp
Apparently has lost his grip
Or what is worse on many views,
Has never had a grip to lose.

The Freudian Complex

The Freudian Complex is a state
Where black is white and love is hate,
And needs analysis to prove
That white is black and hate is love.

The Noble Gesture

The Noble Gesture
Is mostly vesture:
What's really him
Is pretty slim.

Youth and Age

The cult of youth means misery for most of life.
"The Clouded Future of the American Economy," 1975,
p. 22.

If we crack the aging barrier, the human race will probably be
faced with the greatest crisis of its existence. The nature of the
crisis can be summarized by saying, who wants to be an assistant
professor for 500 years?
"The Prospects of Economic Abundance," 1967, p. 48.

By the time a youth group has succeeded in winning something
from the middle-aged, its members are likely to be middle-aged
themselves and suffering from their own earlier success.
Conflict and Defense, 1962, p. 200.

By taking children off their parents' hands and by moving
young people off the streets and into high schools and colleges,
the schools perform a public service somewhat akin to the gar-
bage collector. They remove sources of disutility and segregate
them away from the rest of society, at least for certain hours of the
day. . . . The willingness of people to raise their school taxes is
remarkably enhanced by a school system shutting down for a few
weeks and delivering the children to the tender mercies of their
parents.
"The Schooling Industry as a Possibly Pathological Section of the American Economy," 1972, pp. 131-132.

"Youth" — a disease which has the great gift of being curable.
"Passages: Work and Aging in America," 1978, p. 4.

The Little Casket Maker's Lament

Words and music by
Kenneth Boulding

Piano arrangement
by Howard Kubik

The obvious life strategy for youth is a long-range project to increase respect for the aged.

>   Comment in class, Feb. 10, 1971.

Young people . . . are more sensitive to the future than oldsters, simply because they are going to live in it longer.

>   "New Goals For Society?" 1972, p. 147.

Death is the specter at every human feast, the fly in every human ointment.

>   "Outrageous Fortune," 1976, p. 4.

Mitosis (The Amoeba Speaks)

Now is my time full come. The tensions rise
To unsupportable heights. My being splits,
Separates and dissolves. Large transverse slits
Divide each module, wheresoe'er it lies.
My genes at peak load faultlessly apprise
Each part to go where once again it fits
In molecules, uniting all the bits,
And I am doubled as the old cell dies.

And then what rapture, what unearthly pains,
What total ecstasy of death in birth
When comes the great divide. Somewhere on earth
I hear that fusion, and not fission, reigns;
They call it sex. I hear it gives some pleasure,
A distant echo of the bliss we treasure.

>   Unpublished, 1975.

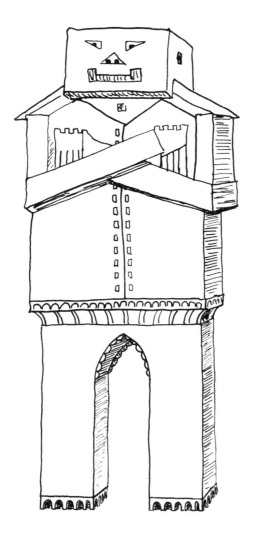

The Monumental Error

The Monumental Error
Is something of a terror,
For when you've gone and made him,
It's difficult to trade him.

The Hidden Motive

Too-curious reader, do not chide
Because the Hidden Motives hide,
But ask yourself, are you quite certain
You want to peep behind the curtain?
And do not, in your virtuous heat,
Mistake Discretion for Deceit.

The Ego

Remarked the Ego to the Id
"I don't approve of what you did!"
The Id to Ego then replied,
"You couldn't even if you tried."
Then interposed the Superego
"Come now, wherever I go, we go."

Education

We have eaten of the Tree of Knowledge, and there is no way back to Eden.... The only recipe for a little learning is a lot of learning. The only cure for the apple is more apple.
> "Dialogue on Peace Research," 1967, p. 9.

The academic world generally goes on the assumption that the more we know of everything the better.... The student has always known better than this. He has usually operated on the principle of knowing as little as he can get away with.
> *The Image,* 1956, p. 162.

Persons who are trained exclusively in techniques prefer to do only the things that can be done with the techniques that they have learned rather than to tackle jobs that may be more important but that are unresponsive to their existing tools, like a surgeon insisting on using his scalpel to dig away a snowdrift.
> "The Task of the Teacher in the Social Sciences," 1969, p. 122.

Perhaps the greatest single defect of our educational organization is that it creates a situation in which the skills of learning and the amount actually learned are competitive goods and in which all the payoffs are for learning something on the spot rather than for acquiring the capability of learning in the future.
> "Some Unsolved Problems in Economic Education," 1971, p. 47.

Physicists and chemists on the whole . . . find it hard to believe they could learn anything from anybody else.
> "Peace Research," 1977, p. 606.

A discipline: An intellectual subculture within which a young person can get recognition and promotion for pointing out successfully where any of his colleagues, particularly his older colleagues, have made mistakes.

> "Peace Research," 1977, p. 604.

I have invented something which . . . I have been calling "Senesh's Law" — that if you can't teach it to the second grade, it probably isn't true.

> "Some Unsolved Problems in Economic Education," 1971, p. 40.

It is the business of professors to be fussy.

> "Justifications for Inequality: The Contributions of Economic Theory," 1975, p. 3.

The academic community . . . is a community singularly free from mortal sin, especially outside the more prestigious institutions where pride has a pretty good following.

> "Scholarly Rights and Political Morality," 1976, p. 216.

We should not despise the ivory tower; for many purposes it is necessary; but we should see that it is provided with good elevator service and that there is a good vulgar TV set in every room.

> "The University, Society, and Arms Control," 1963, p. 463.

A good deal of sociology is devoted to confirming glimpses of the obvious.

> Comment in class, March 31, 1970.

> Schools are designed to serve the youth
> So most of their financial ills
> Come from one sad but basic truth,
> It is the old who pay the bills.
>
> Excerpt from "Verses from the National Institute of Education Meeting," unpublished, 1975.

Disappointment, failure, and frustration are the main agents of change. Success is a poor teacher, for it usually only confirms us in what we thought we knew already.

"Peace Research," 1977, p. 611.

Taxonomy is usually a convenience of the human mind rather than a description of reality.

"Twelve Friendly Quarrels with Johan Galtung," Review of Johan Galtung, *Essays in Peace Research,* Vols. I and II, 1977, p. 78.

The sociology of knowledge . . . became a refugee from Germany along with a number of other distinguished ideas and settled down at the University of Chicago, where to the best of my knowledge, it has been living quietly ever since.

The Image, 1956, p. 150.

The graduate student who confirms, in a new way, the images of the professors is praised for his originality.

The Image, 1956, p. 171.

It may be fine for philosophers "not to do anything, but to observe everything," but if everybody is a philosopher not very much will be done.

The Meaning of the Twentieth Century, 1964, p. 66.

People who know all the answers do not make good teachers. Their own closure closes off the student's mind. It is those who know the questions rather than the answers who are the great teachers.

Review Symposium (with others) of William Breit and William P. Culbertson, Jr., eds., *Science and Ceremony: The Institutional Economics of C.E. Ayres,* 1977, p. 660.

The evolutionary race goes to the adaptable, not to the well-adapted, to those who can learn, not to those who know.

"The Future of Personal Responsibility," 1972, p. 359.

X Cantos

On Learning the Mathematics of Linear Programming

Canto I.

How pleasant it can be to sit
And contemplate the infinite!
The more so, when we recognize
It's only zero in disguise.

Canto II.

The integers march by in fine
Unending, but still counted, line
And in between them march the class
Of fractions in a solid mass.
Then in the holes that don't exist,
Between the fractions, we must list
Uncountable irrational hosts
Of infinitely slender ghosts,
While somewhere in the endless sky
Imaginary Numbers fly
Illumined by the ethereal sun
Of the square root of minus one.

Canto III.

Now, climbing up the mental stairs,
Numbers go by in ordered pairs,
Or, (having no bisexual scruples)
In threes or fours, or in n-tuples.
And so we see (in words director)
That *marriage* is a kind of *vector*
(Though here some varying views prevail
On which sex forms the head, or tail).
Vectors have length and pure direction
And multiply by sheer erection.
They add themselves, like pulling horses,
In parallelograms of forces.

Canto IV.

Between two points lie lots of stations
Called convex linear combinations,

Like intermediate stops that lie
Between two railroad termini
(With three points, now, the combination
Defines a neat triangulation)
And generalizing this, we get
The notion of a convex set.

Canto V.

The extreme point, like young Jack Horner,
Sits lonely in a kind of corner,
And therefore has no points as brothers
That sit with it between two others.

Canto VI.

Take any set, or thing, or crowd,
And wrap it in a kind of shroud.
Then when the shroud is tight and full
We see it as a *Convex Hull.*

Canto VII.

If S and T are convex sets
Their *intersection* then begets
Another set of convex kind.
(Not so, their union, we find
For unions, strangely, may beget
A wholly unparental set.)

Canto VIII.

These theorems are neat and true,
But do they have an end in view?
They do indeed, so let us sing
The Praise of Linear Programming!

Canto IX.

There is a field a point is on
Surrounded by a polygon,
The sides of which, he plainly sees,
Are linear inequalities.
For these expressions (more or less)
Are fences that he can't transgress.
Within the polygon we get

The *feasible* (well-corralled) set.
The problem now, if not the moral,
Is *where,* within the fence, or corral,
A roving point (or wandering beast)
Can get the furthest north-northeast.

Canto X.

I do not want to spend my days
In writing out the i's and j's,
Yet i's and j's are an enigma
When squashed into a double sigma.

Published, 1969.

The Undigested Remark

The Undigested Remark
Is doomed to constant frustration,
Because he feels in the dark
About his communication.

The Boxit

The great advantage of the Boxit,
Is that no misfortune shocks it,
But it must pay for this placidity
By shocking lack of sensitivity.

The Bleary Dither

I'm glad I'm not a Bleary Dither:
He knows not why, or whence, or whither,
Or how, or when, or who, or where;
His mind is neither here nor there.

The Absolute Dirge

Oh, never succumb to the urge
To encounter the Absolute Dirge,
Who totally loses control
In the sensitive searching of soul.

Society

In upper class cultures . . . telling lies and getting away with it has been almost the essence of social intercourse.
"The Specialist With a Universal Mind," 1968, p. 652

Society's "shalt nots" are the fences we erect to keep people from the cliff's edges. Falling over cliffs is the worst possible method of learning about them. The trouble is that in the past we have built fences where there are no cliffs. This deception has given society's taboos their bad name — so much so that many people say no cliffs exist.
"The Power of Negative Thinking," 1978, p. 5.

The ritual element of social intercourse, in taking food and drink together and in conversation . . . may be interpreted as a device to protect us from the awful fate of having to know one another.
Conflict and Defense, 1962, p. 95.

A team sport is a ritual dialectic. It does not really matter who wins, but everybody has to pretend very hard that it does. If it ever really mattered who won . . . one team would poison the beer of the other.
"This Sporting Life," 1977, p. 4.

Freedom is what's inside the fence
Of Morals, Money, Law, and Sense,
And we are free, if this is wide
(Or nothing's on the other side).
We come to Politics (and Sin)
When Your fine freedoms fence Me in,

And so through Law we come to be
Curtailing Freedom — to be free.
Principles of Economic Policy, 1958, p. 110.

The weakness of pure individualism is that there are no pure individuals.
"Man as a Commodity," 1972, p. 48.

Law is the institutionalization of negative thinking.
"The Power of Negative Thinking," 1978, p. 5.

A great problem of the human race at the present moment is that the world is becoming a single ecosystem, but is not a single community. . . . A lifeboat that is not in some sense a community will not bring its human freight to shore, even if there is food for all; for collective decisions will have to be made and, if there is no community, they will not be made and the lifeboat will end up like Lebanon, with a community falling apart and everybody throwing everybody else overboard. We cannot assume, therefore, even if the resources are sufficient for the trip that the trip will be accomplished safely in the absence of community.
"Commons and Community: The Idea of a Public," 1977, pp. 289-290.

Today sex is about as sacred as a common cold and about as mysterious as a gourmet cookbook.
Ecodynamics, 1978, p. 336.

Identity failure is the greatest source of human pollution.
"Towards a Twenty-First Century Politics," 1972, p. 319.

The fact that the news reflects catastrophes, disasters, accidents, wars, and disturbances in a much larger proportion to other events suggests at any rate that these things are relatively scarce and infrequent and that good things are not reported simply because they are common and dull. When a newspaper reports only good news, that is the time to get really worried, for this will suggest that bad news is too commonplace to be reported.
Stable Peace, 1978, p. 83.

Equality is thought up by intellectuals. The plain fact is that ordinary people do not care much about equality. They would rather

have a society in which they have a small chance of being rich than in a society in which they have no chance of being rich.
"Justifications for Inequality: The Contributions of Economic Theory," 1975, p. 13.

If we had a law that anybody who drilled a dry oil well would be shot, very few wells would be drilled. Our tolerance of dry wells does not seem to extend to research projects, which are always expected to gush; to doctors, whose treatments must always cure; to teachers, who must never fail a student; and to manufacturers, who must never sell a defective product. So it may be that the epitaph of our society will read: "Died of extreme accountability."
"Doers and Stoppers," 1975, p. 8.

Septic tanks . . . tend to fill up and overflow and to pollute the whole underground water system, and the same may be true of the social septic tanks implied in the segregation and neglect of the poor, the old, or the mentally and morally ill.
"Man as a Commodity," 1972, p. 47.

Justice . . . It is an invisible perfume in the air; it seems to lie thicker in some places than in others.
"Reflections on Law and Justice," 1978, p. 11.

There are three major patterns of coordination, which I have dubbed the "three P's": prices, policemen, and preachments. Prices, of course, is the market, which coordinates the diverse values of individual buyers and sellers, producers, and consumers into a set of outputs and prices. . . . Policemen means politics, that is, legitimated threat and the organizations which are based on it. . . . Preachments is a symbol of a moral order characterized by ethical ideas and communication.
"Do the Values of Science Lead to a Science of Value? " 1978, pp. 549-550.

A marriage in which all the talk is of obligations rather than of love is on its way to the divorce court. The church in which all worship is obligatory is on its way to abandonment or reformation, and the state in which service has become a duty is in no better case.
"The Impact of the Draft on the Legitimacy of the National State," 1967, p. 195.

The weak have nowhere to go, no place to which to retreat, and their very weakness makes their bargaining commitments irrevocable. Thus, the sick, the aged, children, and the insane have society by the throat; their weakness gives them an unshakeable bargaining position. They say, in effect, "Support us, or we die, and our blood will be on your heads." Because of their weakness, this is no idle threat.

Conflict and Defense, 1964, p. 315.

Law is concerned mainly with the redistribution of old rights and properties, and surely if it were staffed with considerably less able minds than it is now, society would be very little worse off.

The Impact of the Social Sciences, 1966, p. 105.

One gets a depressing feeling sometimes that the people who are most admired by mankind and who are regarded as its heroes are precisely those who have created the maximum amount of human misery. . . . Those who have made things a little better for little people — the traders, the producers, the inventors, even the bankers — have no monuments and receive no eulogies.

The Economy of Love and Fear, 1973, p. 99.

The existence of strain and the existence of positive probabilities of breakdown into open conflict must inevitably produce professionalization of people whose prime business is to engage in conflict when it occurs. The professional success of these people, however, depends on conflict, and they have a professional interest in maintaining conflict, at least at the level where their services are perceived to be required.

Stable Peace, 1978, p. 50.

Never underestimate the power of hypocrisy. Hypocrisy is one of the principal origins of social change. Without hypocrisy, we probably would not have any social change at all. If we were not hypocritical about the race problem in this country, we would not have any movement in the direction of integration.

"The War Industry and the American Economy," 1970, p. 15.

The law . . . is only necessary at the edges of society where custom crumbles, and where the taboos that enable us to live together begin to break down. Thus, one sees the law not so much as the walls of the human household as the weatherstripping and the roof repair.

"Reflections on Law and Justice," 1978, p. 12.

Notes on Emancipation

Where can the Heavenly Kingdom come,
If not among the HUMANUM,
Or, more impressively, Humanum,
(That's Man, and all things that consarn' im)?

Yet Man, it seems, today is fated
To be wholly emancipated,
And live in worlds that he creates,
In Social-Democratic States.
The Monarchs all have had their fling,
So God must be deposed as King,
And be elected President
Of the Republic Firmament,
Where Angels lose their lordly nature,
And Man controls the legislature.
Not even Heaven can afford
The Image of a Feudal Lord,
And Gabriel will have to lump it
Now Man can blow the fatal trumpet.

For Man can make and Man can figure,
His itchy finger's on the trigger;
Unshackled from all bind and baffle,
With Science as his bit and snaffle,
Man casts aside the Primal Curse
And breaks and rides the Universe,
And with the Bomb to hang his fate on,
He must be either God or Satan.

Yet, in the moment of his power
Man finds the taste grow strangely sour,
And in the world that he has made
He trembles, lonely and afraid.
His much admired emancipation
Leads into deeper alienation.
Still lingers on the Primal Curse;
His Revolutions make things worse,
He split the atom far too soon,
Pollution spreads from Earth to Moon,
Youth finds itself soon over thirty,

And Art grows dull as it grows dirty.
He finds himself left in the lurch
By Partner, Party, State, and Church,
Surprised to find his trust betrayed
By every idol he has made,
For Power, with only Man as Master,
Serves but to damn him all the faster.

He shouted "Get your hands off me!"
To God, King, Lord, and Bourgeoisie,
But shudders, as his world grows dim
To find his own hands laid on him.
And so, as man becomes his maker,
The goods he makes can find no taker.
And as he totters to his fall
He cries "God save us!" after all.

Unpublished, 1968.

The Unmitigated Nuisance

I have not known just what to do since
I met the Unmitigated Nuisance,
Even although she only dwells
Within the Imagination's cells.

The Feedback

The Feedback lives upon its tail,
A source of food that cannot fail,
For Messages that bear repeat'n
Will grow as fast as they are eaten.

The Intervening Variable

The Intervening Variable,
Thinks his life will be more stable,
If his features he ensconces
In Stimuluses and Responses.

Ethics and Common Sense

Hatred injures the hater as well as the hated. Love blesses the lover as well as the loved. This is hard economics as well as good ethics.
> "The Economics of Human Conflict," 1965, p. 191.

I don't really believe in "doing good," because that's insulting to the people you're doing good to.
> "The Clouded Future of the American Economy," 1975, p. 34.

Language deludes us into thinking that our linguistic categories are more uniform than in fact they are. The great semantic formula, "this is not that" — this trade union is not that trade union, this Jew is not that Jew, this communist is not that communist, this fascist is not that fascist — is a very important litany which can save us very deep and painful misunderstandings if it is practiced carefully.
> *Ecodynamics,* 1978, p. 54.

Anything worth doing is worth doing badly.
> *Creative Tension,* 1974, p. ix.

The Second Law of Practically Everything: that all things slide down towards a middle muddle unless somebody does something about it. (Note: elsewhere called "The Law of Moth and Rust.")
> "Discussion" (of Allen V. Kneese's "Environmental Pollution: Economics and Policy"), *American Economic Review,* 1971, p. 167.

We tend to overestimate the success of heroic behavior because it is only the successful heroes that we hear about. The unsuccessful ones are quietly buried.

> "The Role of the Church in the Making of Community and Identity," 1969, p. 2.

In the case of highly complex realities . . . ignorance, if not bliss, is at least cheap.

> "Toward a Theory of Discrimination," 1976, p. 12.

If there is a tiger in the room . . . the man who doesn't see it is just about as well off as the man who does. Indeed, it may well be that the man who doesn't see the tiger has the best chance of survival. He will not be paralyzed with fear, he will not attract the tiger's attention, and by going about his own business quietly, he may escape the destruction which his more knowing fellow invites by the very effects of his knowledge. We cannot rule out the possibility that under some circumstances, ignorance is bliss, and knowledge leads to disaster.

> *The Image,* 1956, pp. 168-169.

The wearing of a halo is a balancing feat of some difficulty.

> Personal letter, 1936 — *Creative Tension,* 1974, p. 136.

We must always be on the lookout for perverse dynamic processes which carry even good things to excess. It is precisely these excesses which become the most evil things in the world. The devil, after all, is a fallen angel.

> "Toward a Theory for the Study of Community," 1972, p. 29.

A threat seldom teaches the threatened what the threatener wants him to learn.

> "Preventing Schismogenesis," 1969, p. 152.

Nothing fails like success, because we do not learn anything from it.

> "What Do Economic Indicators Indicate?: Quality and Quantity in the GNP," 1971, p. 78.

Burning convictions have often led to the burning of people, the philosophy of mutual toleration seems to have much to recommend it, even if it leads to some loss in intensity.

> "Toward a Theory of Discrimination," 1976, p. 11.

It is not always unreasonable to be unwilling to receive a gift horse without looking it in the mouth.
The Economy of Love and Fear, 1973, p. 15.

The "sour grapes" principle — we decide that we don't really want what we persistently don't seem able to get.
"Reflections on Law and Justics," 1978, p. 12.

The second fiddle is an instrument on which a lot of beautiful music can be played.
"The Role of the War Industry in International Conflict," 1967, p. 59.

Preferences about other people's preferences . . . might be described as first-order ethics.
"Notes on Goods, Services, and Cultural Economics," 1977, p. 12.

Love

Love is not an engine
It pulls no train of cars
But it draws us all towards itself
And leaps among the stars.

Love is not a weapon
It has no power of threat
And yet it is a sharper sword
Than any wielded yet.

Love is not a method
It has no subtle skill
And yet it is the only way
To carry out the will.

Love is not a policy
To choose to gain an end
But it causes seeds of fear and hate
To flower into a friend.

For Love can only be itself
It is no other thing
Yet of all other ends and means
It is the crownless King.

Unpublished, 1973.

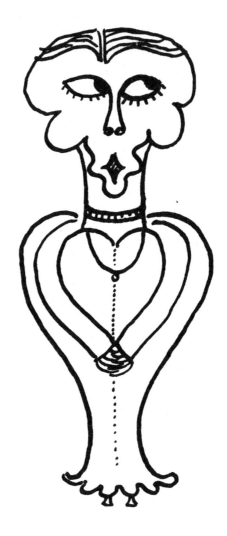

The Priss

The habitation of the Priss
Is seldom an abode of bliss,
For Happiness would not intrude
Upon such total rectitude.

The Sloom

The air of supernatural gloom
That veils the features of the Sloom,
Is but a pose, for truth to tell
He likes himself extremely well.

The Donna

If you should chance to come upon a
Loud and active Concert Donna,
Be sure to stuff your ears with cotton,
Once heard, she is not forgotten.

Truth and Knowledge

Boulding's first law is that anything that exists is possible. It is surprising how many people do not believe this.

    "The War Industry and the American Economy," 1970, p. 15.

There is a famous passage in Sherlock Holmes where the good Watson reproves the Master for his ignorance of astronomy, and Holmes defends himself by saying that he cannot afford to carry any surplus knowledge in his profession, and that the question of whether the sun goes round the earth or the earth goes round the sun is a matter of utter indifference to him. In that argument I confess I am on the side of Watson! There are things which we should know simply because of our status as men.

    "The Knowledge of Value and the Value of Knowledge," 1959, p. 40.

Truth has two meanings. On one hand it is the opposite of lies, and on the other hand it is the opposite of error.

    "Dialogue on Peace Research," 1967, p. 27.

I accept the limitation of the traffic light. We all stop for a red light. This is a limitation of our freedom, but we accept it because we recognize that it is a limitation which in effect produces more freedom. If we did not have any traffic lights we should probably be dead, and there is nothing less free than being dead.

    "Economic Libertarianism," 1965, p. 40.

Faced with homeostatic failure, the schizophrenic adjusts his perceptions, the weak man hauls down his ideals, and the hero puts

in a new furnace and insulates the house. The wisdom of the spirit consists in the knowledge of the proper proportions of these three responses — the blind eye, the struck flag, and the renewed effort.
"Social Justice in Social Dynamics," 1962, p. 79.

Triviality is the ritual that protects us against the abyss of love.
Conflict and Defense, 1962, p. 95.

We assume that everything in a pigeonhole is a pigeon, when in fact all pigeonholes contain a vast variety of birds, and even a vast variety of pigeons.
"Guilt by Association," 1977, p. 3.

The "Pinocchio Principle": Someone sets up what is supposed to be a puppet and it starts to walk. The church-founded college starts to behave like a college and eventually it breaks its church connection. The subsidiary takes off on its own and may buy itself back from the mother company and become independent. The colony may have a revolution and become another nation.
"Intersects: The Peculiar Organizations," 1973, p. 183.

Reality is that image which gets you into less trouble than others.
Comment in class, Spring 1971.

Truth and error grow side by side, like the tares and the wheat.
The Impact of the Social Sciences, 1966, p. 9.

In the last analysis it is love, not money, that makes the world go round; even though money is certainly useful for greasing the axle.
Review of Milton Friedman, *Capitalism and Freedom,* 1963, p. 121.

He whose heart is pure has the strength of ten; but if he doesn't know what to do, he will be terribly dangerous.
"Dialogue on Peace Research," 1967, pp. 27-28.

Freedom, if I may be pardoned for parodying Holy Writ, is power, law, and understanding; and the greatest of these is understanding.
"The Dimensions of Economic Freedom," 1964, p. 122.

Superstition . . . is the perception of patterns where there are none.
Ecodynamics, 1978, p. 9.

There is a profound asymmetry between truth and lies, in the sense that lies can be found out whereas truth cannot. . . . If our image of the world is that we can fly by flapping our arms when we jump off the Empire State Building, the real world will break into our illusions with considerable rapidity. Superstition may be long lived, but truth is immortal.

> *Ecodynamics,* 1978, pp. 236-237.

The trouble with half truths . . . is the other half.

> "Defense and Opulence: The Ethics of International Economics," 1951, p. 210.

The trouble with taxonomic boxes . . . is that they tend to be empty, however beautiful they are on the outside.

> "The Intellectual Framework of Bad Political Advice," review of W.W. Rostow, *Politics and the Stages of Growth,* 1971, p. 604.

The real name of the devil is *suboptimization,* finding out the best way to do something which should not be done at all. The engineers, the military, the governments, and the corporations are all quite busy at this.

> "Fun and Games With the Gross National Product: The Role of Misleading Indicators in Social Policy," 1970, p. 170.

Nothing destroys legitimacy like being found out in a lie.

> "Some Hesitant Reflections on the Political Future," 1970, p. 204.

The price of ingenuity is the toleration of evil.

> Excerpted from "Notes From Woods Hole," unpublished, 1976.

There is a universal principle, Murphy's Law: "If anything can go wrong, it will." I was in Ireland a couple of years ago, and heard a corollary to that, called O'Toole's Law, which says that Murphy is an optimist.

> "The Next 200 Years," 1976, p. 159.

The only unforgivable sin is despair, because it is so completely self-justifying.

> "The Future of Personal Responsibility," 1972, p. 353.

The greater the power we have, the greater our affluence, the more important it is to ask ourselves the fundamental questions as to what it is all for, as to what *we* are all for, as to what we want anyway ... Even if these questions can't be answered ... this is still no excuse for not asking them.

"Where Do We Go From Here, If Anywhere?" 1961, p. 72.

Ballad of Philosophers

Philosophers are never slow
To talk of what they do not know.
They range the countries of the Mind
In search of what they cannot find,
Dashing along in hot pursuit
Of the elusive Absolute
Oblivious of the fact, one fears,
That it has been extinct for years.

And so the words fly to and fro
Like arrows from a doughty bow
Which, fired completely in the dark,
Too seldom seem to find a mark.
These words indeed exhibit strength
In inverse function to their length.
And those not feathered out with wit
Are grounded long before they hit.

The questions, as they come and go,
Were asked a long, long time ago
Like what, and why, and where is Man,
And is he part of any plan?
And what is good, and what is bad,
And who is sane, and who is mad?
The questions all are very clever
But answers seem remote as ever.

Prince, if you are indeed of Peace,
Make words as well as wars to cease
When they are used in man's affairs
As weapons, not as messengers.

Unpublished, 1968.

The Incipient Harangue

When you foregather with the gang,
And spy the Incipient Harangue,
Interpret it as time to leave
And you will rarely have to grieve.

The Triangular Cliché

The brash Triangular Cliché
Is usually in the way,
And is, when trying to be eternal,
A nuisance transient and infernal.

The Affable Doak &
the Bibulous Wunket

The Affable Doak and the Bibulous Wunket,
Love to go off by themselves on a junket,
But no matter how great the restraint
    they display,
They always regret it the following day.

Economics, the Economy,
and the Economic Man

People are the only major product that is produced by largely unskilled labor.

> "The Household as Achilles' Heel," 1972, p. 111.

Economics without sociology is almost skeletal; especially since becoming mathematized it has lost contact with the real world. It deals too much with x and y and not enough with English sheep and French wine, local carpenters and wide-ranging truck drivers.

> Review of Richard A. Peterson, *The Industrial Order and Social Policy,* 1973, p. 555.

> Our policy, to be effective,
> Must chase a suitable objective,
> So, our economy should be
> Both Growing, Stable, Just, and Free.
> The Dog would surely be a Dunce.
> Who tried to chase four things at once,
> Yet this is just the way we plan
> The task of Economic Man!
> *Principles of Economic Policy,* 1958, p. 1.

There is a famous character in one of Oscar Wilde's plays who knew the price of everything and the value of nothing. An economist wonders uneasily if the reference is not to him.

> "Some Contributions of Economics to the General Theory of Value," 1956, p. 1.

The GNP neglects household production and only includes items in the market. If a man marries his housekeeper, the GNP falls; I argue that if he is a moral man the GNP ought to rise because he is enjoying all he had before and then some.

"Fun and Games with the Gross National Product: The Role of Misleading Indicators in Social Policy, 1970, p. 162.

In a world of technicians, it is the economist who raises the cry that the technically most efficient is not necessarily, or even usually, the socially most efficient; that the best cow is not the one that gives the most milk; the best business is not the one that makes the most profits; the best army is not the one that creates the most havoc; and, above all, the best training is not the best education.

"Is Economics Necessary?" 1949, p. 240.

Without the free spirit, affluence is only a form of slavery to undisciplined desires.

"Where Do We Go From Here, If Anywhere?" 1961, p. 72.

> Businessmen are rather dumb,
> Their model is a rule of thumb.
> Economists, it should be said,
> Prefer to have a rule of head.
>
> But when the head is blank inside,
> The thumb at least can hitch a ride,
> And so one model comes in view —
> To do what all the others do.

Excerpted from "Arden House Poetry," 1963, p. 369.

Capital is merely human knowledge imposed on the material world.

"Twelve Friendly Quarrels," Review of Johan Galtung, *Essays in Peace Research,* Vols. I and II, 1977, p. 82.

(On the reliability of National Income Statistics)
One gets an uneasy feeling sometimes that these numbers are simply made up by a little man with a green eyeshade in the attics of the Department of Commerce.

"The Need for Reform of National Income Statistics," 1971, p. 95.

Farmers, as a result of a long process of natural economic selection, acquire a genius for getting into debt at the wrong time.
> "Economic Analysis and Agricultural Policy," 1947, p. 445.

The way to be rich is to be virtuous, saving, thrifty, and inherit a department store!
> "Justifications for Inequality: The Contributions of Economic Theory," 1975, p. 7.

> The Farmer is obsessed with Price:
> So Parity's his pet device;
> But now, alas, we find in Parity
> The nation's most expensive charity.
> Those generous contributions which
> Should help the Poor, support the Rich,
> Because, when Prices we uphold,
> We pay the more, the more is sold.
> *Principles of Economic Policy*, 1958, p. 313.

Byronic frenzy may inspire us to say, "Let joy be unconfined"; the economist says, "You'll have to pay for this tomorrow."
> "Is Scarcity Dead?" 1966, p. 36.

It is clear that economists have a fair amount of narcissism and that they like thinking about themselves and writing to each other about themselves, without a great deal of reference to the outside world.
> "The Misallocation of Intellectual Resources in Economics," 1971, p. 42.

It took the bankers twenty years to catch up to the fact that we were having inflation — which is about right for bankers.
> "Has the Wind Turned Against Us?" 1978, p. 50.

What the economist calls an equilibrium of behavior, psychologists tend to call frustration.
> *The Economy of Love and Fear*, 1973, p. 97.

"Know whom" is a fantastically important capital good.
> "Justifications for Inequality: The Contributions of Economic Theory," 1975, p. 8.

Economists . . . think that factors of production are land, labor, and capital. . . . These are medieval aggregates with all the scientific validity of earth, air, fire, and water, and . . . the real factors of production are know-how, energy, and materials.

> "Has the Wind Turned Against Us?" 1978, p. 45.

There is danger . . . that people will take economic behavior as the measure of all things and will confine their relationships to those which can be conducted on the level of the commercial abstraction. To do this is to lose almost all richness or purpose in human life. He who has never loved or has never felt the call of a heroic ethic — to give and not to count the cost, to labor and not to ask for any reward — and has lived far below the peak levels of human experience. Economic man dwells in Limbo — he is not good enough for Heaven or bad enough for Hell.

> "The Principle of Personal Responsibility," 1954, p. 7.

The role of economists in the world today . . . is almost distressingly like that of the bishops in the British House of Lords or the cardinals in medieval European courts.

> "Scholarly Rights and Political Morality," 1976, pp. 205-206.

[A] . . . source of frustration in the demand for justice is what I have called the illusion of the pie. This is a metaphor beloved by economists — that there is a static pie of goodies which is divided among the members of the society, presumably by a rather skillful wielding of knives. . . . Reality is much more complex. There is no single pie, but there is a vast pattern of little tarts, each growing or declining at its own rate. The growing ones get richer; the declining and stationary ones get poorer.

> *Stable Peace,* 1978, p. 76.

(Note on the relevance of the field of International Trade Economics)
It is evident that we are dealing with an arbitrary and almost meaningless segment of the universe, much as if we had set up a Study of Things Beginning with P, and written textbooks around peanuts, politeness, and peculiar people.

> "Defense and Opulence: The Ethics of International Economics," 1951, p. 210.

The only final good is the quality of human life.

> "Love, Fear, and the Economist," 1973, p. 38.

Ditchley Park Anthology:
Minutes in Verse

Minutes of
Session I:

Decisiveness in Signaling is good
When we decide things rightly (as we should)
When we decide things wrongly, as we do,
The foot, somehow, is on the other shoe.
A hundred years ago the Bank said "Hi!"
Men jumped, and passed quite good investments by,
Today, Authorities say vaguely "'lo!"
But what it means, why, no one seems to know.

Minutes of
Session II:

The Integration of European Capital Markets

In cents and dollars, pounds and pence,
There is a Liquid Turbulence,
And large financial integration
Leads to excessive speculation,
Whereas in Marks and Francs and Lira,
The market's smaller, trade is dearer,
So European Gnomes or Elves
Expend their savings on themselves —
Though people now are growing fond
Of Eurodollar and Eurobond
For Love of Money Finds a Way
When Greeks and Arabs come with pay.

If capital is free to flow,
The State may find itself in tow
(Humiliating Circumstance!)
Behind the Tug of High Finance.
With many hands on many tillers,
And ten Charybdises and Scyllas,
And strong Propensities for Wrecks,
The wonder is we save our necks,
And yet the politicians shudder
To think of one hand on one rudder,
Because nobody can agree
On whose the guiding hand should be.

So Integration, all can see,
Is Good — for everyone but me.

Do flexible exchange rates spell
Descent into some kind of hell?
No, when exchange is Freed, man rises
To high Miltonian Paradises,
Where Trade is obviously meant
To substitute for Government,
And the whole Universe is planned
By Heaven's non-existent hand.

Minutes of
Session III:
Issues Emerging from Money and Growth Models

The models of demand for money,
Combined with interest rates and growth
Produce conclusions mildly funny,
And to accept them I am loath.
Forgetting things at constant rates
Is not the thing I do at all;
My youth in detail I relate,
But yesterday I can't recall.

Money is something of a veil —
Though of what temple is not clear,
And growth is such a long, long tale
There is *no* star by which to steer.
And interest is a neat device
To part the owner from control;
Equations are extremely nice,
But Truth is an elusive goal.

Minutes of
Session IV:
Recent Experiences in the Use of Fiscal Policy

For the first hundred years, you loot your
National domain of gold and land,
And then you mortgage all your income's future
In hope of making money-stock expand.

Churchill and Keynes played fugues upon the organ

Of Fisc and Tax — we all are overjoyed,
Except, perhaps, friends of the House of Morgan —
At filling forests with the Unemployed.

So we set up a Cybernetic System,
Pacemaker for the Economic Flutter,
But how to *test* when we have hit or missed 'im
Is fortunately not *my* bread and butter.

Authorities can't hope to solve the riddle
Of how to chase four rabbits at a time,
And so the Quality of Nero's fiddle,
Does not become the topic of my rhyme.

Yes, Multiple Objectives are a curse,
Yet are, perhaps, not totally appalling:
Who fires his shotgun at the Universe
Can always point with pride to something falling.

Though Policy may follow Fillip's Law —
Too little and too late, too much, too soon;
Last night a man-made satellite I saw:
There is *some* sense in crying for the moon!

Minutes of
Session V:
How Does Monetary Policy Affect the Economy?
(A Shakespearean Sonnet, as Written
by Swinburne and W.S. Gilbert)

We must have a good definition of Money,
For if we do not, then what have we got,
But a Quantity Theory of no-one-knows-what,
And this would be almost too true to be funny.
Now, Banks secrete something, as bees secrete honey;
(It sticks to their fingers some, even when hot!)
But what things are liquid and what things are not,
Rests on whether the climate of business is sunny.
For both Stores of Value and Means of Exchange
Include, among Assets, a very wide range,
So your definition's no better than mine.
Still, with credit-card-clever computers, it's clear
That money as such will one day disappear;
Then, what isn't there we won't have to define.

Minutes of
Session VI:
How Did the New Economics and the New
View of Monetary Institutions Fare in
the Light of 1966 and 1967 Experience?

When money flows into the market jungle
To what part of the forest does it go?
Perhaps the reason why we sometimes bungle
Is that we really do not know.
Though lots of cash, for each man very nice is,
He goes to market and says "buy, buy, buy!"
But this inflates — we don't know quite *what* prices,
Although we think we do know why.

Bankers are terrified of price inflation:
That's odd; for them it pays off fairly well.
Economists, in less protected station,
Don't care so much, or else don't tell.

Who pays for war, apart from those who fight it?
Savings and Loan, and those who might have built?
When fruit is sour, whose teeth have got to bite it?
On whose establishment the guilt?

One answer lies in intermediation —
Which means, who gets crunched when there is a
crunch.
So, having solved the problem of inflation
We cheerfully adjourn for lunch.*

*Poetic License — we actually adjourned
 for coffee.

Minutes of
Session VII:
International Liquidity

There's a solution now to man's equations,
Though stocks are still and flows are all too runny
To Mondialize the cities and the nations
And Mundellize the money.

To peg or what to peg, and at what prices —
That is the question, and indeed the rub
Which hangs less on ingenious devices
Than on who's in whose club.

The purpose of a stock of liquid assets
Is to prevent adjustments, in the main,
So, when the question's seen in all its, facets
We can Allay our pain.

The use of gold for money is in trouble
Because there's something good as gold, or better
That's not invented yet — so should we double
The cost of our gold fetter?

Epilogue:
Farewell to Ditchley Park

The conference is over — it remains
In suitable and Decametric strains
To sing the praise of noble Ditchley Park
That on our mem'ry now has made its mark.
For this great house, without a vulgar note —
Its welcome dignified, but not remote,
Praise will not do — we need a better verb,
So LAUD the fare, both English and Superb,
And MAGNIFY the house where HODSON's reign
And BURDEN lifts all burdens in his train.

Published, 1969.

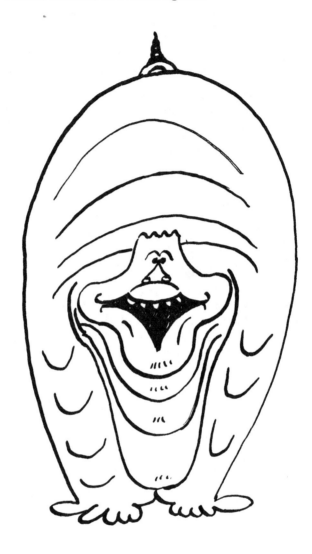

The Unspeakable Doach

The Doach embodies Coarse Delight
In gratifying Appetite,
So take him as a Role, to see
Exactly what you should not be.

The Pirsel

The evolution of the Pirsel
Encountered once a strange reversal,
Retreating at a frightening rate
Towards the Vegetable State.

The Piffle

The Piffle is so very small
He hardly can be seen at all,
Even through microscopic lenses,
And yet his life's as full of frenzies
Of pride and anger, hope and fear
As if he were as big as we are.

Corporations and Other Organizations

One of the problems of large organizations is that it is difficult to keep large purposes before the minds of small people.
Conflict and Defense, 1962, p. 161.

There is a bank in Michigan which had a motto, "The Bank That Puts People First." I have never believed this; if I believed it, I would take out my money and put it in another bank. I do not want a bank to put people first; I want it to put money first.
"Economic Libertarianism," 1965, p. 38.

The committee . . . is the altar at which the rites of persuasion are mainly performed. Show me an organizations without committees and you will show me one without persuasion.
"The Ethics of Persuasion," unpublished, 1971, p. 13.

The lust for life even in organizations is very strong. It is even becoming an increasing problem for persons, as we find that the medical profession is increasingly devoting its expensive energies towards keeping alive people who, though it seems harsh to say it, would be better off dead. One wonders if the financial intravenous feeding that seems necessary for Amtrak does not have a parallel in our best hospitals.
"Intersects: The Peculiar Organizations," 1973, p. 188.

It is always easier to get people to pursue the interesting than the important.
The Impact of the Social Sciences, 1966, p. 113.

Collective bargaining . . . is often a phony bargain. What labor, for instance, gains in wages is not at the employer-bargainer's expense, but at the expense of those who must pay a higher price for the product, and who are not at the bargaining table. Collective bargaining, with all its contributions to industrial jurisprudence, is also a system of taxation without representation.

"Inflation and the Social Contract," 1976, p. 3.

A square person in a round role may become a little rounder, but he also makes the role squarer.

"General Systems Theory: The Skeleton of Science," 1956, p. 205.

In a hierarchy there is an inescapable tendency toward pleasing the superior, and hence confirming his own ideas. Hierarchy in organizations, therefore, produces a condition akin to paranoia in individuals. The information-gathering apparatus always tends to confirm the existing image of the top decision-makers, no matter what it is.

"The Learning and Reality-Testing Process in the International System," 1967, p. 10.

A man rises, on the whole, by pleasing his superiors. At the top this ability is useless. A man who rises to the top . . . by pleasing his superiors is apt to find himself ill-adapted to the role that he finds there.

"The Future Corporation and Public Attitudes," 1963, p. 174.

The greatest dilemma of the corporation, especially the large corporation, is that it is all too likely to have expelled for insubordination at the age of thirty, the man who ought to be its president at the age of fifty-five.

"The Future Corporation and Public Attitudes," 1963, p. 174.

Antitrust legislation has never achieved any coherence and . . . it often gives one the impression of a knight in shining armor mounting his white horse and riding off in all directions at once.

"The Changing Framework of American Capitalism," 1965, p. 41.

> Business is a useful beast,
> We should not hate it in the least;
> It profits should not be sequestered,
> And yet it should be mildly pestered.
> To pester, rather than to bust,
> Should be the aim of Anti-Trust
> For business best can serve the nation
> When pushed by gentle irritation.
>
> *Principles of Economic Policy,* 1958, p. 285.

There is a fundamental distinction perhaps between the challenger and the dissenter. The challenger sets out to create a new orthodoxy; the dissenter cannot really bear the loss of something to dissent from, and hence would not really want to destroy that from which he dissents even if he could.

> "A New Look at Institutionalism," 1957, p. 2.

Both the persistence of hereditary monarchies over hundreds of years and the equally persistent democratic conviction that any fool can be President indicate a certain superiority of the role over the particular individual who occupies it.

> *The Organizational Revolution,* 1953, p. 80.

The fact that powerful people tend to be in their sixties, indeed, puts a sharp time horizon on their decisions — "après moi le déluge" is a state of mind by no means confined to Louis XV.

> "Bottleneck Economics," 1974, p. 16.

> One rule emerges with precision
> That I don't have a crush on —
> The less important the decision
> The longer the discussion
> We tear our hair and beat our breast,
> Because, no doubt, we should.
> But constant searching for the Best
> May overlook the Good.
>
> Excerpted from "Notes From Woods Hole," unpublished, 1976.

Decisiveness is often considered a virtue in hierarchies and a reputation for decisiveness leads to promotion. Decisiveness, however, may be learned through simple good luck, and the people who tend to get promoted are often those who are both decisive and lucky. When we get into higher positions, however, decisiveness is much less of a virtue, and luck may run out.

"Quality of Life and Economic Affluence," 1974, p. 89.

The Brandywine River Anthology

I

The main objective of Du Pont
Is making things which people want,
Perhaps not giving too much thought to
Whether folks want just what they ought to!

II

John, who's hard working and inventive,
Gets bonuses as an incentive:
But how does this affect morale
In Joe, his underserving pal?

III

In modern industry, research
Has come to be a kind of Church,
Where rubber-aproned acolytes
Perform their Scientific Rites,
And firms spend funds they do not hafter,
In hope of benefits Hereafter.

And yet, by far the greater part
Of Chemistry is still an Art;
In spite of scientific fuss
Research is just a blunderbuss,
Which shoots a monstrous charge of shot,
And sometimes hits, but mostly not.

IV

In every giant corporation
Are channels of communication,

Along which lines, from foot to crown,
Ideas flow up, and vetoes down.

V

Polyamides and Polyesters
Make money for Du Pont Investors,
And incidentally, are giving
Us better things for better living.

VI

Du Pont's capacity to Plan
Includes the Suit, but not the Man.
Only philosphers suppose
That man's created by his clothes.

VII

In modern corporate enterprise
Prices are fixed by compromise,
Not, as the college student learns,
By maximizing net returns.

VIII

In spite of all the salesman's lure,
There's just no way of being sure:
One never knows what's gained or lost
In undertaking selling cost.
One pays for Operatic Soap
In Faith, and is returned in Hope
And yet, though knowledge equals nought,
There still is one consoling thought,
That when the selling budget waxes,
A lot of it comes out of taxes.

IX

People above the Second Grade
Seldom require the Visual Aid.
The chart, that eye can not quite reach,

Is not a substitute for speech,
And folks are seldom made to laugh
By diagram or flannelgraph,
And don't accept with gratitude
The List, served up with platitude.
But gladly under him they sit
Whose information's spiced with wit,
Whose face bespeaks a good digestion,
Whose mind is quick to catch a question,
Who keeps all crutches at a distance,
And speaks his piece without assistants,
Using the blessed power of speech
To learn himself, as well as teach.

X

A man of vision in his day
Was Eleuthère Irenée
It was a most prophetic font
At which was named this first Du Pont.
For far across the western seas
Were Eleuthèrian Mysteries —
That means, translating something quick,
That *Liberty* can do the trick,
For Liberty, combined with pluck,
Adding no doubt a dash of luck,
Has fathered mighty enterprises
Producing fabulous surprises,
Too many, indeed, to keep a file on —
Explosives, lacquers, rayon, nylon,
Outdoing silkworm, sheep, and spider
In fields forever growing wider,
And making (without ever cheating)
Old mother nature take a beating.

Nor do prophetic voices cease,
For Irenée, in Greek, means "Peace,"
A curious name, perhaps, to find,
In merchants of — Oh, never mind.
And yet this prophecy runs true;
The turning stage brings into view
A curious transformation scenic,

From Arms of War to things Irenic,
As Mars, whose name they used to call on,
Gives place to Venus dressed in Orlon.
Once more the mighty words we say
Of Eleuthère Irenée,
Du-Pont — which mean, to those who heed 'em
A sort of Bridge to Peace and Freedom.
This bridge, though very strong and wide
Does not quite reach the other side:
Technology and Enterprise
Stop slightly short of being wise
To where they really ought to go;
This interrupts the traffic's flow,
And lands us in a deep frustration,
Dangerous to Company and Nation.

The Engineer, with head undented,
Is always product-oriented,
It's true he gives us Better Things,
Riches more vast than ancient Kings,
But even creaseless Dacron suits
Are but imperfect substitutes
For quiet lives and peace of mind,
And — nightmare thought — suppose we find
That this perfection in production
Leads us to ultimate destruction,
Whether by large or little doses,
By Bomb, or ulcer and neurosis.

The moral of this sort of stuff,
Is, Chemistry is not enough,
There must at least be some reliance
On Fundamental Social Science.

XI

The Boss should neither be a brute,
Nor yet a father substitute,
And should remember, if he can,
That Employee is also Man.
Treating him well just makes him wild,

If he is treated as a child.
He loves, of course, his Country Club
And Welfare Schemes — but here's the rub,
They will not have a good effect
Unless he keeps his self-respect.
                    Moral.
The Best Industrial Relations
Involve two-way Communications.

XII

It is a little odd that Sales
Are generally made by Males,
Whereas by far the largest spender
Is of a wholly different gender.

XIII

The Chemists, at Niagara Falls
Take Salt and rend its parts asunder —
But still, outside the flaming walls
The Falls excite the greater wonder.

XIV

Du Pont has done us very well,
It keeps an excellent Hotel,
It plies us well with food and drink
And even tries to make us think.
But as in all fields Good Relations
Involve two-way Communications,
The question rises into view,
What can Professors do for You!
We therefore strongly recommend
That soon, Du Pont should start to spend
A million bucks (it won't be missed!)
Upon the Social Scientist.
Your pure research in Chemistry
Paid off, as anyone can see:
Might not a similar alliance
Do likewise, with pure social science?

You have your Social Engineers
Who take their problems by the ears
But there is something to be said
For taking problems by the Head,
And though results might not be visible,
At least the Idea isn't Risible.

Published, 1958.

The Drumble

The Drumble hardly ever sins,
For when he runs he only spins,
And so, not getting any place,
He hardly ever falls from grace.

The Inflationary Spiral

The horrid Spiral is unending:
He feeds on Deficits and Spending,
And ever round and round will drift
Till stopped by Taxes or by Thrift.

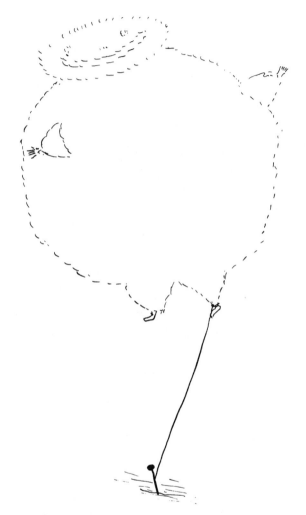

The Fuff

The difficulty of the Fuff
Is that he does not weigh enough:
He might be cured if he would stop
Subsisting on Meringue and Pop.

Government and Politics

Democracy is Government by Squawk.
> "Parity, Charity, and Clarity: Ten Theses on Agricultural Policy," 1955, p. 3.

In the United States . . . we seem to have a very fundamental principle, that while we are willing to spend a lot of money to see that public funds are spent honestly, we will not spend a dollar to see that they are spent wisely.
> "The Relations of Economic, Political, and Social Systems," 1962, p. 359.

The only thing that prevents planning from being disastrous in government is that it is not usually believed.
> "Reflections on Planning: The Value of Uncertainty," 1974, p. 8.

The precision rifle rather than the blunderbuss is what is needed; nevertheless, it must be admitted that most action leans to the side of the blunderbuss. This is particularly true of governments, whose general response to trouble is to fire off a monstrous charge of legislative or military shot and hope that at least something hits somebody.
> *The Organizational Revolution,* 1953, p. 71.

I've been propounding what I call the law of political irony: almost everything we do to help people hurts them and everything we do to hurt people helps them.
> "Love, Fear, and the Economist," 1973, p. 33.

I am almost certain the government has not reached the point of doing more good than harm. Every time Congress adjourns I draw a huge sigh of relief in that a damaging process has been temporarily suspended.

"What Can We Know and Teach About Social Systems?" 1968, p. 3.

The individual gives up a great deal in terms of being taxed, conscripted, killed or injured in wars, and burdened with the guilt of murder and destruction; in return the state seems to give him little, except perhaps a bit of security and a larger identity. It is not surprising, therefore, that we are urged to ask not what our country can do for us, but what we can do for our country. The first question might prove to be too embarrassing.

"The Boundaries of Social Policy," 1967, p. 7.

Except for national defense, the Federal Government is almost unnecessary in this country! . . . If it disappeared, we would not notice it in Colorado for weeks!

"Justifications for Inequality: The Contributions of Economic Theory," 1975, pp. 11-12.

Our record with regulation is, I would say, on the dismal side of neutral.

"Dialogue: Civilized Society," 1975, segment 25.

We seem increasingly to be moving toward a point where the legislature decides that something should be done and the executive decides what.

The Organizational Revolution, 1953, p. 181.

> The reason why cities are ugly and sad
> Is not that the people who live there are bad;
> It's that most of the people who really decide
> What goes on in the city live somewhere outside.

"What Can We Know and Teach About Social Systems?" 1968, p. 3.

The nice thing about the War Against Poverty is that nobody lost it.

"Justifications for Inequality: The Contributions of Economic Theory," 1975, p. 6.

It is clear that public goods are much more like Christmas presents than they are like purchases, that is, they involve reciprocity rather than exchange, and just as one seldom gets what one wants for Christmas, one seldom gets what one wants from taxes.

"The Need for Reform of National Income Statistics,"
1971, p. 95.

A bandit who wants to get a grant regularly, must become either a tax collector or a landlord, and his "victim" must be elevated to the status of taxpayer or renter.

"The Grants Economy," 1969, p. 4.

The dictator... sits in a dark room looking at the world on what he thinks is a television screen, but is actually an old movie, made out of his preconceptions and previous conclusions.

The Organizational Revolution, 1953, p. 65.

It is a misfortune that Departments of Agriculture, Labor, and Commerce were ever organized; there is plenty of opportunity for the expression of group conflicts within the legislative branch of government without deliberately introducing them into the executive.

The Organizational Revolution, 1953, p. 129.

Corruption is the market economy operating in political life.

"Economic Libertarianism," 1965, p. 34.

> It's wise to use the Public Purse
> To Wheedle rather than Coerce,
> And so the self-restraint exhibit
> To Regulate and not Prohibit;
> Because, when things are going slick,
> The Carrot can supplant the Stick,
> Till, in the glare of Fortune's Frown,
> The Stick comes up, the Carrot down.

Principles of Economic Policy, 1958, p. 159.

Legitimacy is like the air that we breathe; we only notice it when it is not there.

"The Role of Legitimacy in the Dynamics of Society,"
1969, p. 1.

He . . . exhibits something of the querulous distemper of the frightened liberal who feels betrayed by everybody and burdened by his own guilt.

> Review of Norbert Wiener, *The Human Use of Human Beings: Cybernetics and Society,* 1952, p. 702.

[The] wide distribution of power may protect against very bad decisions, at the cost of assuring there will be no exceptionally good ones.

> "Determinants of Energy Strategies," 1977, p. 21.

A license is always a poor substitute for a liberty.

> "The Role of the Price Structure in Economic Development," 1962, p. 38.

The Feather River Anthology

I

Reflections on the State, Especially the State of California

A curious creature is the State;
It must persuade — but may dictate;
It has an intermediate station
Between the County and the Nation,
That is, a sort of middle level
Between the Deep Sea and the Devil.
It is its custom and its wont
To do what other people don't.
Its functions, therefore, though official,
Are always somewhat interstitial.

II

On the General Absence of People-Centered Policies

The Army Corps of Engineers
Insists on building Dams and Weirs,
The Reclamation men assume
That *every* desert ought to bloom.
The wildlife people often wish
That all the world were game and fish.
The conservationist's a whiz
At keeping nature as she is.
The Church is measured by its steeple —
And no one gives a dam for people!

III

Ode, on the General Subject of Water

Water is far from a simple commodity,
Water's a sociological oddity,
Water's a pasture for science to forage in,
Water's a mark of our dubious origin,
Water's a link with a distant futurity,
Water's a symbol of ritual purity,

Water is politics, water's religion,
Water is just about anyone's pigeon,
Water is frightening, water's endearing,
Water's a lot more than mere engineering,
Water is tragical, water is comical,
Water is far from the Pure Economical,
So studies of water, though free from aridity
Are apt to produce a good deal of turbidity.

IV

By Friday, in Los Angeles,
A man's mind all a jangle is,
So, to restore his sense of humor
He spends a week end at Cachuma,
Where, for a dollar (less a quarter)
He plays on other people's water.
This recreational ablution
May save him from an Institution,
And is a solid source of wealth
That should be charged to Mental Health.

V

All benefits that are dispersable
Should be, perhaps, non-reimbursible
But people should be made to pay
For benefits that come their way —
Unless we want to subsidize
The good, the needy, or the wise.
(It would be well to be quite sure
Just who *are* the deserving poor,
Or else the state-supported ditch
May serve the Undeserving Rich).

VI

(Chorus of Angelenos, testifying before
Assemblyman Porter's Committee): Agitato

Water, Water,
Mr. Porter,
Save us, Save us,

Mrs. Davis,
O Committee,
O have pity,
Legislator
Do not wait or,
We'll be Thirsty,
Hot and Dirty.
By Anno Domini (Sotto Voce)
2030.

(Mrs. Davis Replies)

Lay no hands on Nature's bounty
In the Northern Mountain County!
Every valiant Northern Daughter
Fights to save her county's water.
What though famine, fire, and drought
Overtake the crowded South,
Water stays for fish to forage in
In the county of its origin!

(Chorus of Committeemen, Maestoso)

To sift the value from the fact
Requires a monumental tact
For values, everybody knows,
Have easy-to-be-stepped-on toes,
And facts so often take a notion
To clothe themselves in wild emotion.

VII

Around the mysteries of finance
We must perform a ritual dance
Because the long term interest rate
Determines any project's fate:
At two percent the case is clear,
At three, some sneaking doubts appear,
At four, it draws its final breath,
While five percent is certain death.

VIII

The Unfortunate Administrator
Is always holding a Hot Potater,

And finds that as a general rule
He cannot wait to let it cool.

The Social Scientist, however,
Can wait around for truth forever,
His problems, then, are self-created
And thoroughly refrigerated.

The Administrator's good digestion
Rests on his answering a question,
But Social Scientists who can, Sir,
Insist on questioning the answer.

IX

Remarked the Bureau to the Corps
"Confine yourselves to flood and war"
Said Engineers to Reclamation
"You are obsessed by Irrigation."

This acrimonious debate
Brings water to the thirsty State,
For mutual recriminations
Are soothed by large appropriations.
And each Congressional Committee
Is moved by pork, if not by pity.

The danger, it is plain to see,
Comes when the Agencies agree,
For what they might agree *about*
Is apt to cause an Urban Drought,
By so pre-empting nature's juices
To strictly vegetable uses.

X

Water is needed for use as detergent
But washing is seldom exceedingly urgent
Water for drinking is all very fine
But Frenchmen get by with the drinking of wine
Water is useful for flushing a toilet,
But sewage is good if you filter and boil it

Water has many industrial uses
But most kinds of cooking can stew in its juices
Water is flexible, water is plastic
And both its supply and demand are elastic
So what is the fuss about, what is the hurry?
And why is this fluid the source of such worry?
The answer, perhaps, will be found in the time it
May take to insure against changes of climate
For water in storage, stashed safely away
Is a rain-day fund for the non-rainy day.

Published, 1966.

The Stuffed Shirt

The Stuffed (and often empty) Shirt
Is difficult to classify:
The Laundry treats him just like dirt,
But Diners rank him very high.

The Smurge

It's odd I never felt an urge
To get acquainted with a Smurge:
I'm told that they are very nice,
And totally immune to vice.

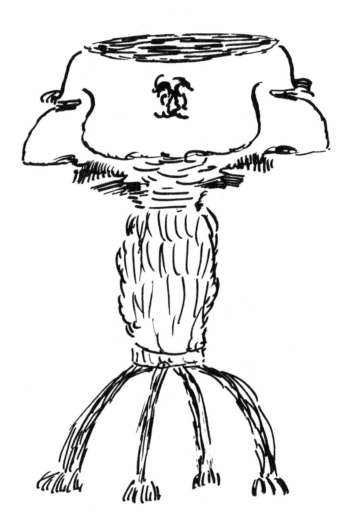

The Two-Faced Whatnot

The Two-Faced Whatnot does not know
Just what he is, or where to go:
It's fortunate that he is able
To find employment as a table.

Capitalism, Communism, and Socialism

Pooh is the almost perfect symbol of what might be called the decent left: furry, attractive, and rather simpleminded about honey.

> "Is Economics Obsolete?" Review of Adolph Lowe, *On Economic Knowledge: Toward a Science of Political Economics,* 1965, p. 139.

Jews, Christians, and Communists see history as a one-way street with a triumphal arch somewhere down the road: as we approach the moment of triumph things get worse all the time, until the end of history and the beginning of the new heaven and the new earth. The Communists and the Jehovah's Witnesses are brothers under the skin, though they would be highly insulted if told so.

> "Economic Theory: The Reconstruction Reconstructed," 1957, p. 43.

Communism is burning down the house to roast a pig. And if you can roast a pig much easier, then it's silly to burn down the house.

> "Dependence and Interdependence as Determinants of Hemispheric Peace," 1978, p. 109.

The fact that revolutionaries are heroes enables them to justify the enormous amount of human misery which they cause, and the fact that bankers are not heroes prevents them from justifying even the inconspicuous but possibly quite large amounts of human betterment which they foster.

> "Introduction," in *Economic Imperialism: A Book of Readings,* 1972, pp. xvi-xvii.

Maoism is how to be poor and like it.
> "Looking Ahead. Interview: Kenneth E. Boulding," 1973,
> p. 492.

You can't exploit anybody as well as he can exploit himself.
> "War as an Economic Institution," 1962, p. 41.

If we list centrally planned economies we have, in order of size,
the Soviet Union, the U.S. Department of Defense and then the
People's Republic of China.
> "Economic Libertarianism," 1965, p. 35.

The moment for socialism passes. . . . Once the moment has
passed and the bus has gone by, if there is a successful process of
capitalist development, the Marxist system becomes increasingly
unrealistic and the socialist alternative increasingly unattrac-
tive. It is one thing to cry "workers of the world unite, you have
nothing to lose but your chains"; it is another to urge the workers
of the world to "unite for you have nothing to lose but your out-
board motors."
> *A Primer on Social Dynamics*, 1970, pp. 88-89.

The Marxist concept that alienation arose when somehow the
workers lost the product of their labor in the great sewer of
exchange has always reminded me a little bit of the psychoanalytic theory that our troubles are due to the fact that our first product was flushed down the toilet.
> *Stable Peace*, 1978, p. 79.

I recall the old joke about capitalism being a system in which man
exploits man, whereas under socialism the reverse is the case.
> *The Economy of Love and Fear*, 1973, p. 63.

If you build a society on the basis of pie in the sky for your grand-
children and you wait long enough, eventually someone will come
along and say "where is the pie?" And if there isn't any pie, you're
in trouble. This is about where the communist world is today.
> "The Real World of the Seventies and Beyond," 1970,
> p. 19.

All economic activity consists . . . in building up little unstable
castles of commodity in the teeth of ceaseless gales of corrosion
and decay.
> Review of Norbert Wiener, *The Human Use of Human
> Beings: Cybernetics and Society,* 1952, p. 702.

Capitalism fails to generate a general loyalty to its own peculiar institutions because these institutions are too rational, too cold-blooded, and do not satisfy the deep desire in human nature for the romantic and the heroic. Hence the bright young men become socialists, and no matter how successful capitalism is, it finally dies of a broken heart because nobody loves it.

"Economic Theory: The Reconstruction Reconstructed," 1957, p. 47.

Abolishing private property does not produce a society in which everybody does things for love. It leads instead to a society dominated by terror at its worst and propaganda at its best.

"Aristocrats Have Always Been Sons of Bitches, 1973, p. 86.

The great political virtue of the market mechanism [is] that it makes political decisions virtually unnecessary and relies on the cumulative impact of the small decisions of little people, which are much less likely to be in error than the large decisions of the great.

"Determinants of Energy Strategies," 1977, p. 20.

The greatest advantage of socialism is that it can exploit the worker much more effectively than capitalism can.... If you want rapid development at all costs, then socialism is fine. On the other hand, though, if you want rapid development cheap, I can get it for you wholesale.

"War as an Economic Institution," 1962, p. 42.

The Composite Varmin

There's no real harm in
The Composite Varmin;
His only vice
Is not being nice.

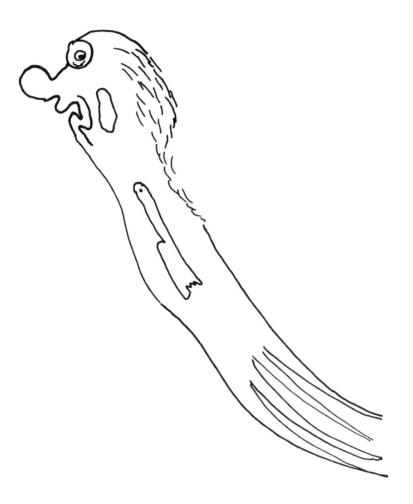

The Back-Eyed Mizz

The misery of the Back-Eyed Mizz
Is quite peculiarly his:
His eye is pale, his cheek is hollowed
Because he fears he isn't followed.

The Pop-Eyed Gloom

I think I safely may assume
You never met a Pop-Eyed Gloom,
And as I do not wish you ill,
I fondly hope you never will.

Foreign Affairs

Our statesmen want peace in very much the same sense that they want a fine day for a picnic. It is a good thing if it comes along, although nobody believes one can really have a policy about it.
"Can There be a National Policy for a Stable Peace?" 1970, p. 172.

Peace is the skillful management of conflict.
"A National Peace Academy?" 1977, p. 22.

Diplomacy is the time when you make the threats of war and war is the time when you have to carry them out because your bluff is called.
"War as an Economic Institution," 1962, p. 44.

The liberal is a man who does not believe in coercion at home, but who does believe in it abroad.
"Economic Libertarianism," 1965, p. 35.

A special form of superstition to which the international system is particularly subject might be called "overlearning." The actual occurrence of a somewhat improbable event always leads to a great overestimation of its probability. . . . Hitler, for instance, may well have been a "thousand-year flood" in the international system — that is, a rather improbable event which actually happened. There are signs indeed that many people in the international system overlearned from this event.
"The International System in the Eighties: Models of International Peace," 1975, pp. 3-4.

The cowboy theory [of revolution] is the theory that people are divided into good guys and bad guys, and that the business of a revolution is to get the bad guys out and the good guys in. It is not always easy to tell the good guys from the bad guys, but, of course, if any guys happen to be on Our Side, they are obviously good, and any guys that happen to be on the Other Side are obviously bad. A good revolution is one in which the good guys beat up the bad guys and a bad revolution is one in which the bad guys beat up the good guys. If there is a good deal of shouting, shooting, and running around going on, preferably on horses, the scenario is regarded as all the more satisfactory.

"The U.S. and Revolution," 1961, p. 5.

Castro . . . is horsing around the world with all the enthusiasm of L.B.J.

"To Cultivate Our Garden," 1978, p. 4.

We must approach history with humility as well as with knowledge, and make policy in meekness rather than in pride. Nevertheless we can cooperate with processes which we do not wholly understand, and as the farmer grows wheat rather than tares without understanding the incomprehensible mystery of the seed, so we can sow peace rather than war, justice rather than injustice, good rather than evil even though both the nature of goodness and the consequences of our acts are only imperfectly understood. In this curious diffident confidence, therefore, we can go forward into policy.

"Economic Theory: The Reconstruction Reconstructed," 1957, p. 23.

I would like to see a United Nations Spying Organization which would spy on everybody and publish the results immediately.

Stable Peace, 1978, p. 118.

The ordinary budget of the United Nations is . . . only a quarter of that of the Department of Sanitation of the City of New York. . . . We get what we pay for, and we get the amount of world peace that we are willing to pay for.

"Economic Libertarianism," 1965, p. 38.

A single world culture . . . has grave dangers. It means that if anything goes wrong, everything goes wrong.

"Foreword," in *Communicating Across Cultures for What?* 1976, p. i.

Ballad of Strategic Studies

Now, in the nuclear age, *intent*
Means more than *capability,*
Which boosts the random element
And damps predictability.
The greater everybody's power
The more important is the *will*
So Rationality turns sour
In the strange world of overkill.

We wait around for Judgment Day,
Our casuistry is Second Best,
Technology goes on its way
And politics become a jest.
Your probabilities are fine
In making conduct rational
But when the death involved is mine
You'd better think again, old pal.

The major virtue of the Czechs
Which should not need apology
Lies in their skill in saving necks
And losing ideology.
When necks have clever heads attached
The ideology is bent,
So Think with Tanks are more than matched
By solid moral armament.

Prince, if you find these lines obscure
It may, alas, be better so
For your disease is hard to cure:
Some things it's better not to know.

Unpublished, 1968.

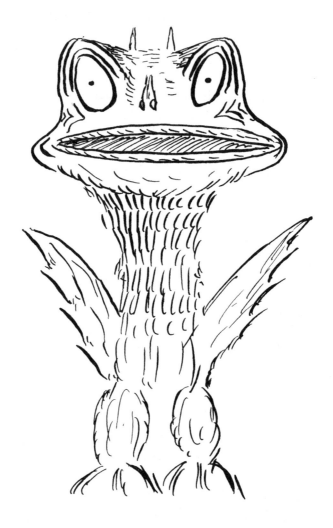

The Wide-Mouthed Goggle

The Wide-Mouthed Goggle, as a bird
Is verging on the Quite Absurd,
And soon would be extinct, by murder,
Were not his foes a shade absurder.

The Snoryena

Perhaps some distant planet teems
With creatures seen in human dreams,
And there they tremble in their boots
When the uncouth Snoryena toots.

The Five-Toed Fuzz

I like to think about the Fuzz
I often wonder what he does,
And what he eats, and where he goes,
On all his five exciting toes.

Nations and History

The belief that history had to happen the way it did is just an illusion of historians. The record is that of a succession of improbable events that somehow came off.

> "Twelve Friendly Quarrels with Johan Galtung," Review of Johan Galtung, *Essays in Peace Research,* Vols. I and II, 1977, p. 78.

Brazil [has] had a glorious future longer than any other country.

> "Knowledge as a Road to Peace," 1971, p. 3.

It is not the noisy revolutions of politics but the silent revolutions of skill that change the course of man's destiny. The rudder and the horsecollar were mightier than Caesar, and the turnip and steam between them changed the face of the earth more than Napoleon. When historians of the future look back to the twentieth century, it will not be the public turmoil and the wars which will attract their main attention. Hitler and Stalin will be seen as disturbances, mere pimples on the changing countenance of time.

> "Economics: The Taming of Mammon," 1956, p. 132.

The ancient Greeks [were] . . . an insufferably superstitious and quarrelsome bunch of slavers with an undeservedly good press.

> "Two Recent Studies of Modern Society," Review of Sebastian de Grazia, *Of Time, Work, and Leisure,* and Hugh Dalziel Duncan, *Communication and Social Order,* 1963, p. 157.

I was in Poland a couple of years ago and someone told me, "Well now, the first thousand years are the hardest."

> "Greatness as a Pathology of the National Image," 1968, p. 39.

Napoleon created Bismarck, Bismarck created Clemenceau, Clemenceau created Hitler, Hitler created the Pentagon, Stalin created the C.I.A. Perhaps one reason for the biblical injunction to love our enemies is that they make us.
Stable Peace, 1978, p. 18.

The English nation probably owes more to Joan of Arc than it does to William the Conqueror. Indeed, if it had not been for Joan of Arc, the English kings would have settled in the more agreeable part of their dominions, namely France, and England would have become like Brittany, a minor province of a great French empire.
"Commons and Community: The Idea of a Public," 1978, p. 290.

We have achieved personal disarmament almost everywhere except in the wild parts of the world like Sicily and Texas.
"Dialogue on Peace Research," 1967, p. 23.

A little over 100 years ago in 1859, the human race, or at least a quarter of it, discovered a huge treasure chest in the basement; we discovered oil and gas. . . . What do we do, of course, when we find the treasure chest? We live it up and spend it. This is precisely what we have been doing, as anybody does when they come into an enormous inheritance. Now all of a sudden we realize that there is a bottom to the barrel.
"Energy and the Environment," 1976, p. 9.

You have to have pretty good brakes in your car in Europe or you find yourself in another country.
"Greatness as a Pathology of the National Image," 1968, p. 38.

The reason the sun never set on the British Empire was that the Lord couldn't trust the British in the dark.
"Ethical Dilemmas in Religion and Nationalism," 1968, p. 8.

Historians are among the major enemies of the human race, interested only in the glorification of war and the despicable concept of national greatness.
"A New Ethos for a New Era," 1970, p. 94.

Human History in a Nutshell

At least, Technology began
With Adam, or·with Early Man,
And even earlier we see
It starting with the Chimpanzee
When first he used a stone or stick
To do things easy, sure, and quick.

But once Earth got the human brain
Things never were the same again.
For knowledge, artifacts, and skill
Grew, independent of man's will.
Fire led to metals, and to cooking,
Which led to planting, and to looking
Round for other things to plant,
Or animals to tame, which grant
Both meat and motion — protein power —
Which led in turn to a great dower
Of food, beyond what farmer eats.
This lead to architectural feats,
For with the extra food, Kings feed
The soldiers and the slaves they need
To fight, to threaten, and to build
Castles and temples, cities filled
With artifacts and artisans.

So knowledge grows until it spans
The world, and then in near defiance
Of Natural Law, explodes in Science!

So man, with Science now apprised
Becomes Post, and Post-Post-Civilized.
No longer tied to horse or ox,
Or creed or culture orthodox,
Man, with his lustful eyes agleam
Breaks into coal, and oil, and steam,
Electric power, and Nuclear Fission,
With Fusion as his latest mission.
Now that he has the power to man it,
He rips the guts from out his planet,

Feeding insatiable tools
With minerals and fossil fuels
From stocks which ultimately must
Be finite in the upper crust.

So, as he messes up his home
A Doomsday is proclaimed from Rome,
With a computer as the chorister,
Conducted by Professor Forrester.
For if man keeps upon his way,
The devil there will be to pay,
And Faustian man, however nifty,
Will get to Hell by 2050.

If there's an answer, then its basis
Must lie in Higher Homeostasis,
For evolution will not come
To simple equilibrium.
So Man, as critic and creator
Must regulate his regulator,
And even take a higher station
To regulate his regulation.

These theorems never quite assume
Just who is regulating whom,
And so there may be sharp debate
On who, or what, will regulate,
But Homeostasis there must be,
Of third, or fourth, or fifth degree,
Bringing, beyond all these degrees,
Man to his senses or his knees.

Unpublished, 1972.

There isn't anything as uncomfortable as the British house. They believe in being uncomfortable.
"Dialogue: Civilized Society," 1975, segment 23.

Every revolution is only half a revolution. A full revolution brings you back to where you were before, from the Czar to Stalin, or from Louis XVI to Napoleon, or from the last Chinese emperors to Mao Tse-Tung.
"Intersects: The Peculiar Organizations," 1973, p. 186.

I would not want to come out for unconsumable food, even though the British have made considerable advances in this direction.
"The Prospects of Economic Abundance," 1967, p. 41.

President Johnson . . . [was] like the man who [was] putting all of his resources into fighting a distant forest fire when his own house [was] burning down.
"Greatness as a Pathology of the National Image," 1968, p. 42.

> In history, the pursuit of wealth
> Has not been aimed at food or health,
> But was directed to besiege
> The citadels of high prestige.
Excerpted from "Goals of Economic Life," unpublished, 1950.

The English language is not so well adapted as the German for saying nothing in particular about things in general.
The Image, 1956, p. 150.

The fact that Lincoln forced the South into the Union has crippled the Federal Government of the United States for a hundred years. Think how wonderful it would be to get rid of all those Southern Senators.
"Greatness as a Pathology of the National Image," 1968, p. 38.

The British Commonwealth is an interesting example of a society united by distances large enough to overcome mutual dislike.
The Image, 1956, p. 147.

A good deal of the success of the United States . . . is due to the fact that the state boundaries were so ridiculous that it wasn't worth bothering to do anything about them.
"Defense Against Unwanted Change," 1974, p. 15.

It seems sometimes as if parameters are most likely to change when we think them to be most stable, and that history is an elaborate practical joke with the predictors as butt.
"In Defense of Statics," 1955, p. 489.

The Wee Sleekit Moose

The Wee (and often Sleekit) Moose
Is not adept at things abstruse,
But loves and pities without end
The things it cannot comprehend.

The Mathematical Model

The Mathematical Model
Can neither talk nor toddle;
Though plentiful his fruits,
He's grounded in his Roots.
His fruit is wholly credible
But not entirely edible.

Homo Genius

The Homo Genius is so bright
He keeps himself awake at night,
But finds, before his life is done,
Two heads are not as good as one.

War and Peace

Peace — that drab girl with the olive-branch corsage whom no red-blooded American (or Russian) could conceivably warm up to.
> "The Domestic Implications of Arms Control," 1960, p. 858.

The guided missile with the nuclear warhead has really done for the national state, even the largest national state, what gunpowder did for the feudal baron. It has destroyed its military viability and if the institution itself is to survive it will have to be profoundly transformed. Thus, after the invention of gunpowder, the feudal baron had to transform himself into a gentleman with an undefended manor house instead of a castle. Similarly, the survival of the national state in the modern world depends on its ability to organize disarmament, for in a world of armed deterrence it will surely be destroyed, simply because its cost of upkeep is so high and its returns in terms of human welfare are so low.
> "Stability in International Systems: The Role of Disarmament and Development," 1969, p. 201.

The great debate on nuclear policy . . . has been going on for the last twenty years in an atmosphere of such intense intellectual radiation that the main product has been nausea.
> "Chartered Journey Through Theories of Deterrence," Review of Philip Green, *Deadly Logic: The Theory of Nuclear Deterrence,* 1967, p. 496.

I have a design, incidentally, for solving the cold war by having the socialist countries incorporate in Delaware. This would take a lot of the emotional steam out of the whole conflict. Poland, Inc.,

139

for instance, would be at least as democratic as General Electric and it could even sell stock in Hamtramck! A corollary to this pipe dream is that General Motors might declare itself the People's Republic of General Motors and apply for a seat in the United Nations.

"Ethical Dilemmas in Religion and Nationalism," 1968, pp. 10-11.

The systems run by fragile men
Are cheaper done by I.B.M.
So man shall reach Elysian shores
When his computers fight his wars.

Excerpted from "Conference on Theory and Method in the Study of Total Societies," unpublished, 1965.

Peace and war are still too much regarded . . . as a random element almost like weather. . . . Our preparations for bad weather do not usually bring it on. . . . Umbrellas and raincoats are perfect examples of wholly defensive weapons which diminish the impact of bad weather but do nothing either to produce it or to make it cease. In the international system, however, our nuclear umbrellas and our organizations of defense actually increase the probability that the bad weather of war will occur. It is as if our umbrellas brought down the lightning upon us.

"Future Directions in Conflict and Peace Studies," 1978, pp. 353-354.

The fatal weakness of strategic thinking . . . is that it operates . . . with an extremely narrow moral agenda.

"Charted Journey Through Theories of Deterrence," Review of Philip Green, *Deadly Logic: The Theory of Nuclear Deterrence*, 1967, p. 496.

I have often compared the peace movement to the labors of Sisyphus — we push the stone uphill and continually it rolls down again and we have to start all over again. But the hill is not infinite and it has a watershed, and one day the stone will roll over the watershed and we will be chasing it instead of pushing it.

Stable Peace, 1978, p. 66.

If you want to get rich, the way to get rich is to stay home and mind your own business, like the Swedes. There is another recipe,

which is to stay home and mind everybody else's business, like the Swiss.
> "The War Industry and the American Economy," 1970, p. 11.

For the United States disarmament would mean a little more luxury. For the Soviet Union it would mean comfort. If the Russians can devote the fifteen percent of their economy that they are now devoting to arms, to consumer goods, at the end of ten years they would have refrigerators, automobiles, ulcers, and all the conveniences, traffic accidents, and luxuries of modern life.
> "War as an Economic Institution," 1962, p. 41.

The Department of Defense . . . has sold national greatness and militarism at least as effectively as Madison Avenue has sold detergents and deodorants. Between the two of them they could probably purify the hands even of Lady Macbeth.
> *Economics as a Science,* 1970, p. 90.

The military virtues of courage and self-sacrifice, real as they are, are merely the reflected colors on the surface of a vast pool of unspeakable filth and human misery.
> *Stable Peace,* 1978, p. 88.

The international system is a little bit like the San Andreas fault under California. This is deterrence which is very much like an earthquake fault; it is stable in the short run, but not in the long. In X years, San Francisco is going to be destroyed if we can't lubricate the fault. In X years, if the present international system continues, our cities are going to be destroyed, just like San Francisco.
> "Our Habitat: The Universe," 1978, p. 11.

We have put $3 million to a disarmament agency in the United States. We have increased the Fish and Wildlife appropriation to $20 million; so that's $20 million for fish and $3 million for peace. But still, this is about our scale of values.
> "War as an Economic Institution," 1962, p. 48.

We want peace, just as we want utopia, just as long as we are pretty sure of not getting it. When the choice is placed before us, however, as it seems to be in the modern world, between utopia, or at least peace, which is something less, or annihilation, our embarrassment may become so acute that we choose annihilation.

Conflict and Defense, 1964, p. 341.

The Anthropologist

The Anthropologist is Racked
With Passion for the Artifact.

The Octoped

You cannot see the Octoped
Because the last of them is dead,
Although — and this may sound absurd —
They are occasionally heard.

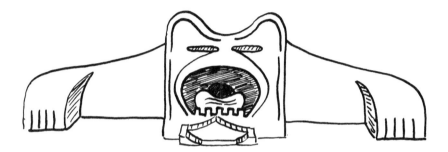

The Architectural Monstrosity

This creature is from granite quarried;
He's very large and very horrid.
A puzzling thought that calls for pity,
Is that his parents thought him pretty.

Science and Technology

Science: the art of substituting unimportant questions which can be answered for important questions which cannot.
> "The Two Cultures," 1967, p. 691.

A legend has it that science is a white knight who lives only in the valley of fact and that philosophy, religion, and the arts are beautiful damsels who live only in the valley of values. . . . As we pursue any value or fact, however, we skirt the valleys of science and values to find ourselves in a bog of ambiguity.
> "Toward a Normative Science," 1977, p. 8.

Technology is the speeding up of the day when everything is gone.
> "Colorado's Kenneth Boulding: A World Renowned Scholar Forecasts Our Future," 1976, p. 48.

(A Small Cry of Distress, from a Not Very Mathematical Man)
> I'm like a rat within a maze,
> When faced with sigma's i's and j's,
> And problems soon become enigmas
> When wrapped in i's and j's and sigma's.
> "General Systems as a Point of View," 1964, p. 25.

The danger of measurement . . . is . . . that we will regard it as truth instead of as evidence.
> "In Praise of Inefficiency," 1978, p. 47.

Architects . . . occupy a traffic island between the sciences and the humanities, participating fully in neither.
> "Dialogue: Civilized Society," 1975, segment 23.

The automobile . . . is remarkably addictive. I have described it as a suit of armor with 200 horses inside, big enough to make love in. It is not surprising that it is popular. It turns its driver into a knight with the mobility of the aristocrat and perhaps some of his other vices. The pedestrian and the person who rides public transportation are . . . peasants looking up with almost inevitable envy at the knights riding by in their mechanical steeds.
    "The Social System and the Energy Crisis," 1974, p. 255.

A somewhat casual observer from outer space might well deduce that the course of evolution in this planet had produced a species of large four-wheeled bugs with detachable brains; peculiar animals which rested when they sent their brains away from them but performed in rather predictable manners when their brains were recalled.
    "Economics and Ecology," 1966, p. 225.

        We cannot walk before we toddle,
        Though we may toddle far too long,
        If we embrace a lovely Model
        That is consistent, clear, and wrong.
    Excerpted from "Notes from Woods Hole," unpublished, 1976.

A computer can be as stupid as it likes because we probably are not going to give it the vote for at least 50 years.
    "Economic Libertarianism," 1965, p. 39.

The atmosphere of the garage . . . is curiously like that of the hospital. The garage is permeated by the same air of professional importance, the same feeling that the customer is rather in the way, the same rather offhand bedside manner, the same assumption that the customer or the patient is, professionally speaking, an ignoramus, if not a fool. In fact, the principal difference between the garage and the hospital seems to be that the hospital is cleaner and more expensive.
    "The Concept of Need for Health Services," 1966, p. 206.

Any statistical analysis can founder on the rocks of parametric shifts, and these rocks are all over the place.
    Comment in class, May 12, 1971.

Physicists only talk to physicists, economists to economists — worse still, nuclear physicists only talk to nuclear physicists and econometricians to econometricians. One wonders sometimes if science will not grind to a stop in an assemblage of walled-in hermits, each mumbling to himself words in a private language that only he can understand.

> "General Systems Theory: The Skeleton of Science," 1956, p. 198.

The organization of science into disciplines sets up a series of ghettos with remarkable distances of artificial social space between them.

> "Foreword," in *Image and Environment,* 1973, p. ix.

The social scientist faces a problem which normally does not bother the nonsocial scientist, in that he is himself part of the field of his investigation. . . . The bacteriologist who must stain his bacteria in order to see them would be in even worse trouble if his bacteria blushed when they were observed.

> "Is Economics Necessary?" 1949, p. 235.

Much of the paraphernalia of science, whether of experiments, sampling, or statistical testing, can be thought of as a kind of ritual designed to protect the scientist against wishful thinking and perception.

> "Twelve Friendly Quarrels with Johan Galtung," Review of Johan Galtung, *Essays in Peace Research,* Vols. I and II, 1977, p. 77.

The computer . . . has given us continuously compounded interest at banks, easier airplane reservations, and a large quantity of unread Ph.D theses.

> "Toward a Modest Society: The End of Growth and Grandeur," 1971, p. 13.

Science has achieved its triumph precisely because it has escaped the swaddling clothes of moral judgment; it has only been able to take off into the vast universe of the "is" by escaping from the treacherous launching pad of the "ought."

> *Economics as a Science,* 1970, p. 117.

It is possible that a new source of bad decisions has been generated in recent years — the illusions of certainty that come with belief in sophisticated, computerized models of the future that do not take sufficient account of the irreducible uncertainties.

> "Determinants of Energy Strategies," 1977, p. 23.

No engineer should be allowed into the world without an ecologist in attendance as a priest.

> "Fun and Games With the Gross National Product: The Role of Misleading Indicators in Social Policy," 1970, p. 169.

The future of science lies in our ability to resolve the ethical conflicts which the growth of knowledge is creating. Science can no longer be objective about what it finds in an unchanging world, because science is no longer merely investigating, it is creating the world it investigates.

> "Colorado's Kenneth Boulding: A World Renowned Scholar Forecasts Our Future," 1976, p. 49.

The Old Agricultural Lag

I

O why does agriculture lag?
The answers all are in the bag
But the bag in which the answer lies
Turns out to have enormous size.

II

The ardent fertilizer buff
Thinks fertilizer is enough
(Such buffs, it's interesting to know
Are much produced in Buffalo).

III

Then some there are who argue that
The major culprit is the rat,
And so encourage, far and wide,
The massive use of pesticide.

IV

Economists, it's plain to see
All think that *Prices* are the key
For no economy will grow
With inputs high and outputs low.

V

Markets and competition now
Must be the hand that speeds the plow
Making, in one Rostovian leap
Corn dear, and fertilizer cheap.

VI

Some think the answer lies in Risk
Others, that land reform's the whisk
To brush away the blocks that bar
Development's immobile car.

VII

Some say, when growth occurs, what fed it
Is careful grants of shaky credit,
With Government to underwrite
The debts of those who fly by night.

VIII

For Anthropologists, Tradition
Remains the major inhibition.
And peasants, oftener than we think,
When led to water, do not drink.

IX

With facts too many now to list 'em
The answer is a General System.
So what has got to be advised,
Is, "get the stuff computerized."

X

When scientists use common sense
They fall into mistakes immense.
It's better far to place reliance
Even on the softest social science.

XI

Hard work and saving à la Mill,
Is seen as far too bitter a pill
So comes the unimplemented plan —
What Mill can't, maybe Millikan.

Published, 1967.

The Random Number

No shreds of dignity encumber
The undistinguished Random Number
He has, so sad a lot is his,
No reason to be what he is.

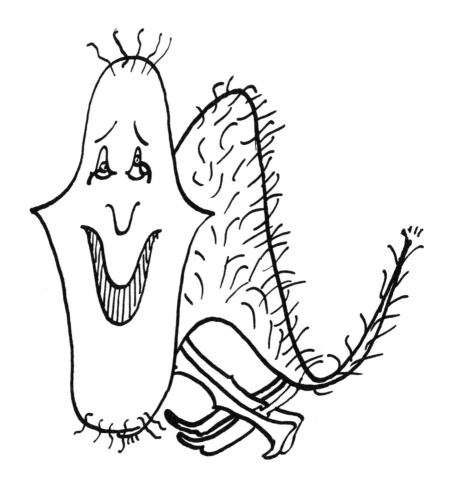

The Stochastic Variable

The wild Stochastic Variable
Is loose, and vague, and quite unstable.
He's so imperfectly located
It's quite a job to get him mated.

The Braided Bunnet

Whate'er he does, the Braided Bunnet
Always wishes he hadn't done it;
Improved would be his sad condition
If only he had less contrition.

Evolution, Ecology, and Spaceship Earth

I am something of an ecologist at heart, mainly because I am really a preacher, and we all know that all ecologists are really preachers under the skin. They are great viewers with alarm. Is there any more single-minded, simple pleasure than viewing with alarm? At times it is even better than sex.

"Fun and Games with the Gross National Product: The Role of Misleading Indicators in Social Policy," 1970, p. 160.

The thing in pollution we most need to know
Is, where does it come from and where does it go?
One major idea in the pot must be tossed,
That things may be missing, but never are lost.
Most chemical elements cannot be changed.
They can't be destroyed, they are just rearranged.
So clean water and air, and, indeed, your clean shirt,
Are obtained by wise segregation of dirt.
So if our research is to bear healthy fruit,
The critical question is *what* to pollute.
One policy matter is clear; the polluter
Should not be allowed to become a commuter.
And as long as industrial systems have bowels
The boss should reside in the nest that he fouls.
Economists argue that all the world lacks is
A suitable system of effluent taxes.
They forget that if people pollute with impunity

> This must be a symptom of lack of community.
> But this means producing a mild kind of love
> So let's hope the eagle gives birth to a dove.
> "New Goals for Society?" 1972, p. 139.

I am not quite sure about evolution before DNA, but I would argue that there are the beginnings of value theory in valency and that carbon has preferences. It is a great, glad-handed rotarian hitching onto everything.

"Comments" (on Roger Troub, "Kenneth Boulding: Economics from a Different Perspective," and on Leonard Silk, "The Economics of Kenneth Boulding"), 1978, p. 536.

I've been going around saying — I'm afraid somewhat to the annoyance of my environmentalist friends, equilibrium is a figment of the human imagination. That is, it is something which hasn't existed, at least in this part of the universe, for at least three and a half billion years if that. . . . Actually, if you want equilibrium, you can go to the moon and take off your spacesuit and then you'll be in equilibrium for another billion years and much good may it do you.

"The World as a Economic Region," 1974, p. 29.

The real difference between an automobile and a horse is that the automobile has a more complicated sex life. A horse and a mare can produce another horse, where two automobiles cannot produce another automobile in spite of all appearances of copulation.

"The World as an Economic Region," 1974, p. 31.

The key word in environmental control is a very unpopular one, that is, "patience." It is impatience that leads to the destruction of the present environment for immediate ends and a neglect of the interests of the future. Impatient young people, therefore, who think that environmental control is something revolutionary and radical, something for which we wave a magic political wand and all our pumpkins turn into effluent-free coaches (and, incidentally, nobody has yet produced an effluent-free horse) are likely to be grievously disappointed.

"Environment and Economics," 1971, p. 367.

One of the odd things about evolution is why it has gone on so long, because you would have thought that any decent world would have stopped with the amoeba. It's an extraordinarily satisfying organism and we've been going into what you might call pathological complexity ever since, ending up, of course, with the Federal Reserve System.

"The World as an Economic Region," 1974, p. 28.

The difference between ecology and economics is the difference between a jungle and a garden; the jungle follows its own latent laws which no participant understands, but man takes these same latent laws and twists them into a garden.

"Economic Theory: The Reconstruction Reconstructed," 1957, p. 25.

We can't anticipate what evolution will bring. I would have placed my money on the cats instead of the apes to have been the source of man. It's obvious that the octopus was a better candidate for intelligence than what was chosen — and it may yet be.

"Colorado's Kenneth Boulding: A World Renowned Scholar Forecasts Our Future," 1976, p. 48.

It is the recurrent catastrophes that permit the meek — that is, the adaptable and the tolerant — to inherit the earth. The strong and the proud — that is, those who are all too well adapted to a particular environment — perish.

"Economic Theory: The Reconstruction Reconstructed," 1957, p. 20.

Blind conservationism ... simply takes the existing distribution of populations, particularly of natural populations, as given, sacred, and sacrosanct. It digs in its heels and regards any departure from the existing world ecosystem as undesirable. ... The logical outcome of this position would be the conclusion that the invention of man himself was deplorable and the only decent thing the human race could do would be to feed itself collectively to the lions and hope the evolutionary process would not make the mistake of creating intelligence of this kind again.

"Economics and Ecology," 1966, p. 232.

Biologists create an aura
Around the fauna and the flora
That are produced in various locuses
By lengthy ecologic processes.
They tend to think that errant Man
Is not included in the plan,
And if he jumped into the lake
Would end Mutation's first mistake.
Excerpted from "Minutes of Meeting of the Seminar on
Man-Environment Relations," unpublished, 1968.

There is a curious illusion today that nature is both wise and good. The awful truth is that nature is a bitch from the human point of view. . . . I care about the whooping crane a little. I would even give $10 to save the whooping crane. The whooping crane doesn't give a damn about me.
"Energy and the Environment," 1976, p. 12.

In the spaceship economy, consumption is no longer a virtue but a vice; and a mounting GNP is to be regarded with horror. . . . Every grain of sand will have to be treasured, and the waste and profligacy of our own day will seem so horrible that our descendants will hardly seem able to bear to think about us, for we will appear as monsters in their eyes.
"Is Scarcity Dead?" 1966, pp. 42-43.

DNA was the first three-dimensional Xerox machine.
"Energy and the Environment," 1976, p. 2.

A species which devotes all its time and energy to subsistence in true Malthusian style will expand to the limit of subsistence where all its energy is devoted to the sheer business of getting a livelihood. Under these circumstances even a minor catastrophe may wipe the species out completely, A species however which develops a certain capacity for "useless" activities — courtship and play — has reserves to fall back on when times get difficult. Man, of course, derives almost all his success from his insensate capacity for plain fooling around. It may be, of course, that this is going to eliminate him eventually, and that his curiosity will one day put an end to itself by putting an end to him. But so far, so good.

> "Economic Theory: The Reconstruction Reconstructed," 1957, pp. 20-21.

I think all good things are artificial. That is, nature ... is cold, miserable, uncomfortable . . . I wouldn't be seen dead in it.

> "Defense Against Unwanted Change," 1974, p. 7.

With development extended to the whole planet earth
What started with abundance may conclude in dismal dearth.
And it really will not matter then who started it or ran it
If development results in an entirely plundered planet.

> "Fun and Games With the Gross National Product: The Role of Misleading Indicators in Social Policy," 1970, p. 170.

The concern for richness and variety of species which leads us to seek to protect the whooping crane and the whale from extinction should also apply to the Amish, the Hari Krishnas, the Fijians, and the Hungarians, without any of which the whole world would surely be poorer.

> "Toward a Theory of Discrimination," 1976, p. 11.

Dirge For an Urban Dweller

I do not really wish to go
And dwell among the Navaho
I have rejected every plan
To live like Neolithic Man
And even when I'm feeling low
I never emulate Thoreau.

The works of Nature in the raw
Are what I have no yearning for
The unexploited wilderness
Is rather an untidy mess
Alas, it cannot be disguised
I dote on being civilized.

I like to drive, I like to fly,
I like ice cream and apple pie
Sometimes, in spite of all derision
I like to look at television
I may be crude, I may be crass
But still I'm fond of Culture (Mass).

I do not feel undue elation
Before climactic Vegetation
Unless the climax that I see
Includes the maintenance of me,
My friends, my children, and my wife
In our accustomed style of life.

And yet I get some inner qualms
From Conservationists' alarms
Perhaps my all too urban race
Has lost its biologic base
And man is clearly understood
To be too clever for his good.

Unpublished, 1970.

A Conservationist's Lament

The world is finite, resources are scarce,
Things are bad and will be worse.
Coal is burned and gas exploded,
Forests cut and soils eroded.
Wells are dry and air's polluted.
Dust is blowing, trees uprooted.
Oil is going, ores depleted,
Drains receive what is excreted.
Land is sinking, seas are rising,
Man is far too enterprising.
Fire will rage with Man to fan it,
Soon we'll have a plundered planet.
People breed like fertile rabbits,
People have disgusting habits.
Moral:
    The evolutionary plan
    Went astray by evolving Man.

The Technologist's Reply

Man's potential is quite terrific,
You can't go back to the Neolithic.
The cream is there for us to skim it,
Knowledge is power, and the sky's the limit.
Every mouth has hands to feed it,
Food is found when people need it.
All we need is found in granite
Once we have the men to plan it.
Yeast and algae give us meat,
Soil is almost obsolete.
Men can grow to pastures greener
Till all the earth is Pasadena.
Moral:
    Man's a nuisance, Man's a crackpot,
    But only Man can hit the jackpot.

Published, 1956.

A Ballad of Ecological Awareness

Ecological awareness leads to questioning of goals:
This threatens the performance of some old established roles.
So to raise the human species from the level of subsistence
We have to overcome Covert Political Resistance.
So we should be propagating, without shadow of apology,
A Scientific Discipline of Poleconecology.

Among the very saddest of developmental tales
Is the indestructibility of fluke-infested snails.
Development is fluky when with flukes the blood is crammed,
So the more we dam the rivers, then the sooner we are damned.

Schistosomiasis has conquered — for the sad Egyptian fails
In six thousand years of history to eliminate the snails;
Yet in spite of all the furor of ecologists' conniptions
The Snail has failed completely to eradicate Egyptians.

In use upon the water of a good molluscicide
We really don't know what is true, but only what is tried.
For snails are pretty clever and climb upon the bank;
So if any good is done at all, we don't know what to thank.

Development must be successful, O, my darling daughter,
So keep your clothes on all the time, and don't go near the water.
The best advice we have is — for developmental tactics,
Don't wash or swim or go to bed without your prophylactics.

Bacteria have learned the trick of formal education —
They can transfer drug resistance with a shot of information.
So perhaps our universities should go in new directions,
And give their education by a series of injections.

The more we move around the world to˙where the prospect
      pleases,
The more we will communicate deplorable diseases.
Yet there may be a solution if we do not choose to flout it,
If we also can communicate just what to do about it.

Development will conquer the diseases of the poor,
By spraying all the houses and by putting in the sewer.

And we'll know we have success in our developmental pitch,
When everybody dies from the diseases of the rich.

The cost of building dams is always underestimated —
There's erosion of the delta that the river has created,
There's fertile soil below the dam that's likely to be looted,
And the tangled mat of forest that has got to be uprooted.

There's the breaking up of cultures with old haunts and habits
     loss,
There's the education program that just doesn't come across,
And the wasted fruits of progress that are seldom much enjoyed
By expelled subsistence farmers who are urban unemployed.

There's disappointing yield of fish, beyond the first explosion;
There's silting up, and drawing down, and watershed erosion.
Above the dam the water's lost by sheer evaporation;
Below, the river scours, and suffers dangerous alteration.

For engineers, however good, are likely to be guilty
Of quietly forgetting that a river can be silty,
While the irrigation people too are frequently forgetting
That water poured upon the land is likely to be wetting.

Then the water in the lake, and what the lake releases,
Is crawling with infected snails and water-borne diseases.
There's a hideous locust breeding ground when water level's low,
And a million ecologic facts we really do not know.

There are benefits, of course, which may be countable, but which
Have a tendency to fall into the pockets of the rich,
While the costs are apt to fall upon the shoulders of the poor.
So cost-benefit analysis is nearly always sure,
To justify the building of a solid concrete fact,
While the Ecological Truth is left behind in the Abstract.

By undiscriminating use of strong insecticide
Our temporary gain is lost when all our friends have died.
With strip planting of alfalfa something new is making sense:
Spend the millions now on tribute — not a penny for defense!

The locust as an insect is extremely international,
It runs a downwind airline, it's adaptable and rational.

For biological controls the beast is far too mobile;
It seems a shame to persecute an animal so noble.
But though the locust is a most engaging little rascal,
I think I'd put my money on Ecology and Haskell.

One principle that is an ecological upsetter
Is that if anything is good, then more of it is better,
And this misunderstanding sets us very, very wrong,
For no relation in the world is linear for long.

Pursuit of agriculture of a lateritic soil
Is a classical example of an Unrewarding Toil,
For the unsuspecting settler gets a very nasty shock
When the lateritic soil turns into lateritic rock.

The poisoned mouse eliminates the useful owl and vulture,
But the growing world economy insists on monoculture.
O! Science may be phony but the social system's phonier,
And so spread on, insecticide, and sulphate of ammonia.

A developed Agriculture is a fabulous polluter;
As development gets faster, then the problem gets acuter.
We are loading up the planet with a lot of nitric trash,
And if nitrogen falls off its cycle — Wow! is that a crash.

Development is fatal to the local and specific;
A single culture spreads from the Atlantic to Pacific.
So preserving every specimen of life is quite essential
If we're not to break the bank of evolutionary potential.

Too many governments, alas, in tropic parts today
Say, "Let us group the little farms," and then say, "Let us spray."
Pests and Pollutions, prosper then, and what is more the pity,
It drives the people off the land to fester in the city.
So how do we inculcate in a heterogeneous nation
The sober sense of ignorance that leads to conservation?

A cost of exercising power is much unwanted heat,
So victory is found to be a species of defeat,
And no amount of slick brochures can cultivate a taste
For dead and tepid rivers and for radioactive waste.

The growth of population has a great deal of momentum,
Neither spirals, interruptus, or safer still, absentum

Can do much about the kids who are already on the scene,
Who will still be in the labor force in twenty seventeen.
So there isn't very much that the developed world can do
To help that poor old woman in the very crowded shoe.

The oceans we have mobilized to feed the too-well-fed;
The rain is red in Adelaide from deserts newly bred;
We nibble at the nomads, though oil-rich and water-poor;
Displaced Masai, domesticated, have a drought in store.

The tsetse fly can guard the wild, as long as it survives;
As men and cattle press the land, the game no longer thrives;
The tourist business is a trap, it is a tainted honey;
Man clearly should have stayed in bed, and not invented money.

It's nice to be the drafter of a well-constructed plan,
For spending lots of money for the betterment of Man,
But audits are a threat, for it is neither games nor fun
To look at plans of yesteryear and ask, "What have we done?"
And learning is unpleasant when we have to do it fast,
So it's pleasanter to contemplate the future than the past.

If it's just the noise of progress that is beating in our ears
We could look beyond the turbulence and soothe our gnawing
    fears.
Man is drowning in his own success, and hapless is his hope
If our science and technology is but a rotten rope.

Infinity is ended, and mankind is in a box;
The era of expanding man is running out of rocks;
A self-sustaining Spaceship Earth is shortly in the offing
And man must be its crew — or else the box will be his coffin!
                                        Published, 1972.

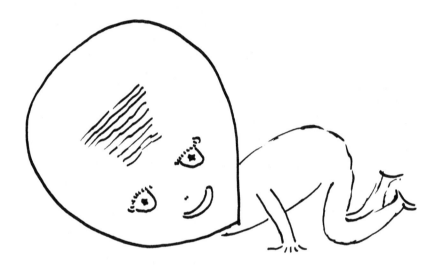

The Liberal Bibb

Whatever happens, do not rib
The ineffectual Liberal Bibb,
Or else his starry eyes will fill
From reservoirs of vague goodwill.

The Bingle

This sorry creature is the Bingle,
His ears and tail and tootsies jingle,
He lives in constant perturbation
Because of Tintinabulation.

The Nosey

The living habits of the Nosey
Are not particularly cosy,
Because he has too much of that
Which is supposed to kill the cat.

The Cutup

It is too bad to have to put up
With all the antics of the Cutup
And everywhere that people gather
He works himself into a lather.

The Future

The person or the nation that has a date with destiny goes somewhere, though usually not to the address on the label.
The Image, 1956, p. 125.

Isaac Watts Revised

What though the mountains are pushed up
By plate-tectonic lift,
And oceans lie within the cup
Made by the landmass drift.
The skies are but earth's airy skin
Rotation makes the day;
Sun, moon, and planets are akin,
And Kepler's Laws obey.

Is it the goodness of the Lord
That fills the earth with food?
Selection has the final word
And what survives is good.
And nature's patterns are displayed
To my observant eye,
The small by microscopes arrayed
By telescopes the sky.

There's not a plant or flower below
But DNA has grown;
And clouds arise and tempests blow
By laws as yet unknown.

However fragile life may be
'Tis in the system's care,
And everywhere that man can be
The Universe is there.

Published, 1976.

In these days one must not despise science fiction as a way of keeping up with the news.

"The Death of the City: A Frightened Look at Postcivilization," 1963, p. 144.

I'm extremely dubious of any projections of the future because of the enormous technological uncertainties. . . . You could have written a beautiful Club of Rome report in the United States in 1858 (you know, the Club of Rome predicts catastrophe and disaster and so on) pointing out that seventy-five or eighty percent of our energy was derived from wood, that we were cutting down our forests at an enormous rate, and that by 1920 or thereabouts it would all be gone. We also could have predicted that New York City would be under fifty feet of horse manure by about the same date.

"Conversation . . . with Kenneth E. Boulding," 1977, pp. 56-57.

In a system of great uncertainty, he who hesitates is frequently saved.

"The Learning and Reality-Testing Process in the International System," 1967, p. 14.

The evolutionary process stopped on the moon some three and a half billion years ago; it got about as far as quartz, and did not go any further because . . . it did not have water, and it is hard to develop complexity without water. As you know, you and I are just water bags of primeval oceans — with a little stiffening, physiologically. There is good reason for this. It is hard to develop complexity in a gas because it is too radical. It is hard to develop complexity in a solid because it is too conservative. But a liquid is just right. Evolution is ballet in water. It may be that we are the intermediary stage between liquid intelligence and solid, going on from transistors and computers. We may be just an intermediary; we may produce our evolutionary successor. I won't like it, because I have a very strong race prejudice; I am in favor of the human race. I am not at all keen on our successor, but I am pretty sure there will be one.

"The Next 200 Years," 1976, pp. 160-161.

The safest way to prepare for the future is to prepare to be surprised, as you surely will be.

"Entropy Economics," 1975, p. 8.

I was recently sitting in an airplane waiting to take off. It was spring and a little bird was trying to build her nest in a little hole at the end of the wing. She flew busily in and out carrying bits of straw and twigs as the plane sat on the ground waiting for the signal to take off, and then the plane roared away and left her far behind. I could not help seeing in this a parable of our day. We are all going about our various tasks, each trying to build for himself a little shelter from the inclement world, a little defense against want or hardship or loneliness, and we are all building on the wings of a great sweeping process of change that may soon roar away with our little efforts, we know not where nor how. There were men in the cockpit, however, and we are men and not sparrows. We do have the gift of understanding, even of the systems that we create ourselves. It is not too much to hope, therefore, that man can learn to fly the great engine of change that he has made and that it may carry us not to destruction, but to that great goal for which the world was made.

Conflict and Defense, 1964, p. 343.

> The only natural resource
> That matters, is the driving force
> That's man's unconquerable itch
> To find, learn, know, adapt, and switch.

"Can There Be A Growth Policy?" 1973, p. 19.

We all know Murphy's Law: that if anything can go wrong it will. Perhaps the fifth law of the universe is: if anything can go wrong, it eventually will. All small probabilities come off.

"Our Habitat: The Universe," 1978, p. 11.

All societies produce effluents of people as of sewage. The criminals, the mentally sick, the self-perpetuating poverty subcultures, and so on. The more complex a society, the more prone it may

become to human effluence; and we may learn that values have to
be recycled just the way nitrogen does.

"The Prospects of Economic Abundance," 1967, p. 53.

The space enterprise has, if anything, accentuated the smallness
of the earth and the loneliness of man. This beautiful blue and
white ball is clearly the only decent piece of real estate in a very
long way and we are stuck with it.

"New Goals for Society?" 1972, p. 147.

The idea . . .that we are about to go forward into a great age of leisure and ultimately machines will do all the work, is a gross fal-
lacy. If this is the Age of Aquarius, it is an irony that this is the
only sign of the zodiac who is doing any work, trudging around
the heavens with his water bucket.

"The Clouded Future of the American Economy," 1975,
p. 26.

One wonders indeed whether the greater orientation to the future
among people living in the Temperate Zone, as opposed to those
in the Tropics, is not due to the experience of the seasons. At the
equator one day is very much like the next. The further north we
go, the more striking becomes the succession of the seasons and
the more aware man is that he is always waiting for something —
"If winter comes, can spring be far behind?"

"The Future as Chance and Design," 1969; *Collected Pap-
ers,* V. 4, p. 528.

> Reality is four-dimensional
> And *some* behavior is intentional
> So hard the task of those who seek
> Maps to the middle of next week.
>
> Mutant ideas, served by Selection,
> Make knowledge grow in *some* direction
> Though it's impossible to know
> In *which* direction it will grow.

Excerpted from "Conference on Theory and Method in the
Study of Total Societies," unpublished, 1965.

Every prediction, like cigarette packages, should have a label
warning: "Believing in this prediction may be injurious to your
health."

"The International System in the Eighties: Models of
International Peace," 1975, p. 3.

One of the most awful truths about the real world is that it is a muddle. Anybody who is clear about it [the world] is under an illusion. However carefully we refine our techniques, we must never desert the great tradition of muddling through. This is the only realistic way to approach the future of anything.

"In Praise of Inefficiency," 1978, p. 48.

Radicals tend to know what they do not want, but not what they do want. They are avoiders rather than approachers, weeders rather than planters.

"To Cultivate Our Garden," 1978, p. 4.

The greatest human tragedy is to feel useless and not wanted, and with the rise in the intelligence of machines, we may face a period in which the human race divides into two parts, those who feel themselves to be more intelligent than machines and those who feel themselves to be less.

"Expecting the Unexpected: The Uncertain Future of Knowledge and Technology," 1966, p. 213.

The vision of the universe indeed as a total system extending magnificently through time and space and with equal magnificence towards the infinitesimal structure, and towards the immense complexity of the inner space of the human mind, is an experience which we need not be ashamed to call religious.

"General Systems as an Integrating Force in the Social Sciences," 1973, p. 966.

One can indeed visualize somewhere at the end of the road . . . a world society with stable population and advanced industrial technology based on solar energy, and the recycling of materials . . . . If this is a pipe dream, let us put a little more into the manufacture of pipes.

"What Went Wrong, If Anything, Since Copernicus ?" 1974, p. 23.

The Wubble

O, how unhappy is the Wubble,
He always finds himself in trouble.
He droops and drips and sobs and splashes,
And lives on sackcloth smeared with ashes.

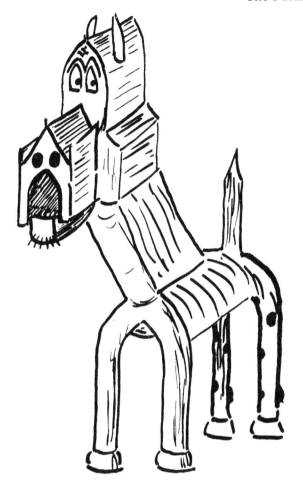

The Gothic Worry

The Gothic Worry has a charm
That comes from never doing harm,
But also, be it understood,
From never doing any good.

The Spherical Wallow

The Wallow is absurdly fat
He will not wear a coat or hat,
Because, he says, they quickly lose
Their shape in the Primeval Ooze.

The Double-Breasted Puffit

The timid Double-Breasted Puffit
Has no conception how to rough it
And only stops his cravings inner
By invitations out to dinner.

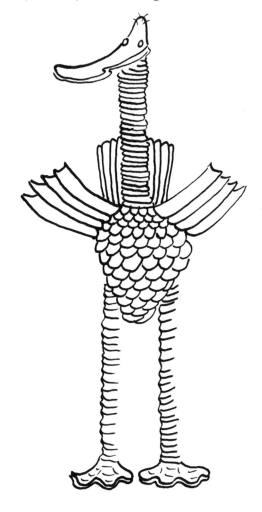

The Baffle

The Baffles, seeking for Defense,
Encased themselves in armor plate.
Alas! It didn't make much sense —
They left no room to propagate.

Sources*

1947 "Economic Analysis and Agricultural Policy," *Canadian Journal of Economics and Political Science,* 13, 3 (Aug. 1947): 436-46. CP I, pp. 219-31.

1949 "Is Economics Necessary?" *Scientific Monthly,* 68, 4 (Apr. 1949): 235-40. BE, pp. 1-13; CP I, pp. 249-61.

1950 "Goals of Economic Life," unpublished verse.

1951 "Defense and Opulence: The Ethics of International Economics," *American Economic Review,* 41, 2 (May 1951): 210-20. CP I, pp. 313-25.

1952 "The Busted Thermostat," verse, *Michigan Business Review,* 4, 6 (Nov. 1952): 25-26.

Review of Norbert Wiener, "The Human Use of Human Beings: Cybernetics and Society," *Econometrica,* 20, 4 (Oct. 1952): 702.

1953 *The Organizational Revolution: A Study in the Ethics of Economic Organization* (New York: Harper & Brothers, 1953; paperback edition: Quadrangle Books, 1968).

*BE: *Beyond Economics,* by Kenneth Boulding (Ann Arbor: University of Michigan Press, 1968; paperback, 1970.)
    CP: *Kenneth E. Boulding/Collected Papers* (Boulder: Colorado Associated University Press, Vols. I and II [edited by Fred R. Glahe], 1971; Vol. III [edited by Larry Singell], 1973; Vol. IV [edited by Larry Singell], 1974; Vol. V [edited by Larry Singell], 1975).

1954 "The Principle of Personal Responsibility," *Review of Social Economy,* 12, 1 (Mar. 1954): 1-8. BE, pp. 210-18. CP IV, pp. 11-20.

1955 "The Conservationist's Lament; The Technologist's Reply," verse, *Population Bulletin* (Aug. 1955): 70; also in *Man's Role in Changing the Face of the Earth,* ed. William L. Thomas, Jr. (Chicago: University of Chicago Press, for the Wenner-Gren Foundation for Anthropological Research and the National Science Foundation, 1956), p. 1087.

"In Defense of Statics," *Quarterly Journal of Economics,* 69, 4 (Nov. 1955): 485-502. CP I, pp. 465-84.

"Parity, Charity, and Clarity: Ten Theses on Agricultural Policy," *Michigan Daily* (Ann Arbor), Oct. 16, 1955, p. 3. CP III, pp. 121-25.

1956 "Economics: The Taming of Mammon," in *Frontiers of Knowledge in the Study of Man,* ed. Lynn White, Jr. (New York: Harper & Brothers, 1956), pp. 132-49. BE, pp. 26-42.

"General Systems Theory: The Skeleton of Science," *Management Science,* 2, 3 (Apr. 1956): 197-208. BE, pp. 81-97. CP IV, pp. 33-46.

The Image: Knowledge in Life and Society (Ann Arbor: University of Michigan Press, 1956; paperback edition, 1961).

"Some Contributions of Economics to the General Theory of Value," *Philosophy of Science,* 23, 1 (Jan. 1956): 1-14. CP II, pp. 1-16.

1957 "Economic Theory: The Reconstruction Reconstructed," in *Segments of The Economy — 1956: A Symposium* (Cleveland, Ohio: Howard Allen, 1957), pp. 8-55. CP II, pp. 35-85.

"A New Look at Institutionalism," *American Economic Review,* 47, 2 (May 1957): 1-12. CP II, pp. 87-100.

1958 "The Brandywine River Anthology," verse, *Michigan Business Review,* 10, 2 (Mar. 1958): 7-9.

Principles of Economic Policy (Englewood Cliffs, N. J.: Prentice-Hall, 1958).

1959 "The Knowledge of Value and the Value of Knowledge," in *Ethics and the Social Sciences,* ed. Leo R. Ward (Notre Dame, Ind.: Notre Dame University Press, 1959), pp. 25-42. CP IV, pp. 85-104.

"Organizing Growth," *Challenge,* 8, 3 (Dec. 1959): 31-36. CP IV, pp. 105-12.

1960 "The Domestic Implications of Arms Control," *Daedalus,* 89, 4 (Fall 1960): 846-59. CP V, pp. 63-78.

"Night Thoughts From My Own Couch," unpublished verse.

1961 "The Little Casket Maker's Lament," unpublished verse.

"The U.S. and Revolution," in *The U.S. and Revolution: An Occasional Paper on the Free Society* (Santa Barbara, Calif.: Center for the Study of Democratic Institutions, 1961), pp. 4-7. CP V, pp. 91-96.

"Where Do We Go From Here, If Anywhere?" in *Proceedings of the Fourteenth National Conference on the Administration of Research* (University Park, Pa.: Pennsylvania State University Press, 1961), pp. 66-72. CP II, pp. 209-17.

1962 *Conflict and Defense: A General Theory* (New York: Harper & Brothers, 1962; paperback edition, 1963).

"The Relations of Economic, Political, and Social Systems," *Social and Economic Studies,* 11, 4 (Dec. 1962): 351-62. BE, pp. 96-111. CP IV, pp. 149-62.

"The Role of the Price Structure in Economic Development," (with Pritam Singh), *American Economic Review,* 52, 2 (May, 1962): 28-38. CP III, pp. 251-63.

"Social Justice in Social Dynamics," in *Social Justice,* ed. Richard B. Brandt (New York: Prentice-Hall, 1962), pp. 73-92. BE, pp. 239-57. CP IV, pp. 163-84.

"War as an Economic Institution," in *The Causes of War,* (Montreal: Sir George Williams University, 1962), pp. 38-48.

1963 "Arden House Poetry," in *Models of Markets,* ed. Alfred R. Oxenfeldt (New York: Columbia University Press, 1963), pp. 369-71.

"The Death of the City: A Frightened Look at Postcivilization," in *The Historian and the City,* eds. Oscar Handlin and John Burchard (Cambridge, Mass.: M.I.T. Press, 1963), pp. 133-45. CP II, pp. 265-79.

"The Future Corporation and Public Attitudes," in *The Corporation and Its Publics: Essays on the Corporate Image,* John W. Riley, Jr. (New York: John Wiley & Sons, 1963), pp. 159-75. CP III, pp. 175-93.

"Review of Milton Friedman, Capitalism and Freedom," *Journal of Business,* 36, 1 (Jan. 1963): 120-21.

"Towards a Pure Theory of Threat Systems," *American Economic Review,* 53, 2 (May 1963): 424-34. CP V, pp. 137-47.

"Two Recent Studies of Modern Society," review of Sebastian de Grazia, *Of Time, Work, and Leisure;* and Hugh Dalziel Duncan, *Communication and Social Order, Scientific American,* 208, 1 (Jan. 1963): 157-60.

"The University, Society, and Arms Control," *Journal of Conflict Resolution,* 7, 3 (Sept. 1963): 458-63; *Journal of Arms Control,* 1, 4 (Oct. 1963): 552-57.

1964   "The Dimensions of Economic Freedom," in *The Nation's Economic Objectives,* ed. Edgar O. Edwards (Chicago: University of Chicago Press, 1964), pp. 107-22. BE, pp. 256-74. CP III, pp. 201-18.

"General Systems as a Point of View," in *Views on General Systems Theory,* ed. Mihajlo D. Mesarovic (New York: John Wiley & Sons, 1964), pp. 25-38. CP IV, pp. 207-22.

1965   'The Changing Framework of American Capitalism," *Challenge,* 14, 2 (Nov.-Dec. 1965): 39-42. CP III, pp. 251-56.

"Conference on Theory and Method in the Study of Total Societies," unpublished verse.

"Economic Libertarianism," in *Conference on Savings and Residential Financing, 1965 Proceedings* (Chicago: U.S. Savings and Loan League, Sept. 1965), pp. 30-42; discussion, pp. 42-57. BE, pp. 41-54. CP II, pp 345-58.

"The Economics of Human Conflict," in *The Nature of Human Conflict,* ed. Elton B. McNeil (Englewood Cliffs, N. J.: Prentice-Hall, 1965), pp. 172-91. CP II, pp. 323-44.

"Is Economics Obsolescent?," review of Adolph Lowe, *On Economic Knowledge: Toward a Science of Political Economics, Scientific American,* 212, 5 (May 1965): 139-43.

The Meaning of the Twentieth Century: The Great Transition, World Perspectives Series, ed. Ruth Nanda Anshen (New York: Harper & Row, 1964; paperback edition, Harper Colophon Books, 1965).

1966   "The Concept of Need for Health Services," *Milbank Memorial Fund Quarterly,* Part 2, 44, 4 (Oct. 1966): 202-25. CP III, pp. 277-98.

"Economics and Ecology," in *Future Environments in North America,* eds. F. Fraser Darling and John P. Milton (Garden City, N. Y.: Natural History Press, 1966), pp. 225-34. CP III, pp. 299-310.

"Expecting the Unexpected: The Uncertain Future of Knowledge and Technology," in *Prospective Changes in Society by 1980, Including Some Implications for Education,* eds. Edgar L. Morphet and Charles O. Ryan (Denver, Colo.: Designing Education for the Future, July 1966), pp. 199-215. BE, pp. 156-75. CP IV, pp. 327-43.

"The Feather River Anthology," *Industrial Water Engineering,* 3, 12 (Dec. 1966): 32-33.

The Impact of the Social Sciences (New Brunswick, N. J.: Rutgers University Press, 1966).

"Is Scarcity Dead?" *Public Interest,* 5 (Fall 1966): 36-44. CP III, pp. 311-21.

"Space, Technology, and Society: From Puff-Puff to Whoosh," Review of Bruce Mazlish, ed., "The Railroad and the Space Program: An Exploration in Historical Analogy," *Science,* 151, 3713 (Feb. 25, 1966): 979.

1967   "The Boundaries of Social Policy," *Social Work,* 12, 1 (Jan. 1967): 3-11. CP IV, pp. 345-55.

"Charted Journey Through Theories of Deterrence," review of Philip Green, *Deadly Logic: The Theory of Nuclear Deterrence, Dissent,* 14, 4 (July-Aug. 1967): 496-98. "Dialogue on Peace Research" (Wallingford, Pa.: Pendle Hill, 1967).

"Evolution and Revolution in the Developmental Process," in *Social Change and Economic Growth* (Paris: Development Centre of the Organization for Economic Co-operation and Development, 1967), pp. 19-29. CP V, pp. 217-29.

"The Impact of the Draft on the Legitimacy of the National State," in *The Draft, A Handbook of Facts and Alternatives,* ed. Sol Tax (Chicago: University of Chicago Press, 1967), pp. 191-96. CP V, pp. 231-36.

"The Learning and Reality-Testing Process in the International System," *Journal of International Affairs* 21, 1 (1967): 1-15. BE, pp. 286-302. CP V, pp. 237-53.

"The Old Agricultural Lag," verse, in *No Easy Harvest: The Dilemma of Agriculture in Underdeveloped Countries,* Max. F. Millikan and David Hapgood (Boston: Little, Brown and Company, 1967), p. xii.

"The Prospects of Economic Abundance," in *The Control of Environment: Discussion at the Nobel Conference,* ed. John D. Roslansky (Amsterdam: North-Holland Publishing Company, 1967), pp. 39-57. CP II, pp. 427-45.

"The Role of the War Industry in International Conflict," *Journal of Social Issues* 23, 1 (Jan. 1967): 47-61. CP V, pp. 255-71.

"The 'Two Cultures,'" in *Technology in Western Civilization,* Vol. II, eds. Melvin Kranzberg and Carroll W. Pursell, Jr. (New York: Oxford University Press, 1967), pp. 686-95. CP IV, pp. 411-22.

1968   "Ballad of Philosophers," unpublished verse.

"Ballad of Strategic Studies," unpublished verse.

"Ethical Dilemmas in Religion and Nationalism," pamphlet, (New York: Ethical Culture Publications, 1968).

"Greatness as a Pathology of the National Image," in *U.S. Foreign Policy: Responsibilities of a Superpower in International Politics* (Champaign, Ill.: University of Illinois Extension in International Affairs, Sept. 1968), pp. 35-42.

"In the Money," review of Ferdinand Lundberg, *The Rich and the Super-Rich;* and Ben B. Seligman, *Permanent Poverty: An American Syndrome, New York Review of Books,* 11, 4 (Sept. 12, 1968): 40-42.

"Minutes of Meeting of the Seminar on Man-Environment Relations," unpublished verse.

"Notes on Emancipation," unpublished verse.

"The Specialist With a Universal Mind," *Management Science,* 14, 12 (Aug. 1968), B-647 to B-653.

"What Can We Know and Teach About Social Systems?" *Social Science Education Consortium Newsletter* (Boulder, Colo.), 5 (June 1968): 1-5; also in *Social Science in the Schools: A Search for Rationale,* eds. Irving Morrissett and W. W. Stevens, Jr. (New York: Holt, Rinehart and Winston, 1971). CP IV, pp. 429-35.

1969   "The Ditchley Park Anthology," *Michigan Business Review,* 21, 2 (Mar. 1969): 17-19; also *Journal of Money, Credit and Banking* 1,3 (Aug. 1969): 354, 462, 507, 555, 624, 681.

"The Future as Chance and Design," in German as "Die Zukunft als Moglichkeit und Design, *Bauwelt 50* (Berlin), 60 (Dec. 15, 1969): 1807-11. CP IV (in English), pp. 525-34. "The Grants Economy," *Michigan Academician,* 1, 1 and 2 (Winter 1969): 3-11. CP II, pp. 475-85.

"Preventing Schismogenesis," *Journal of Applied Behavioral Science,* 5, 2 (Apr./May/June 1969): 151-53.

"The Role of Legitimacy in the Dynamics of Society," pamphlet (University Park: Pennsylvania State University Center for Research, College of Business Administration, 1969). CP IV, pp. 509-23.

"The Role of the Church in the Making of Community and Identity," pamphlet (Greeley, Colo.: First Congregational Church, 1969).

"Some Unsolved Problems in Economic Education," in *Five Levels of Incompetence: Report of the 1969 Grove Park Institute,* ed. Thomas Vogt (Washington, D.C.: Consortium of Professional Associations for Study of Special Teacher Improvement Programs (CONPASS), 1971), pp. 37-50.

"Stability in International Systems: The Role of Disarmament and Development," in *International Security Systems: Concepts and Models of World Order,* ed. Richard B. Gray (Itasca, Ill.: F. E. Peacock, 1969), pp. 193-210. CP V, pp. 353-72.

"The Task of the Teacher in the Social Sciences," in *The Quest for Relevance: Effective College Teaching; Vol. III, The Social Sciences* (Washington, D.C.: American Council on Education, for the American Association for Higher Education, Mar. 1969), pp. 3-24. CP IV, pp. 469-90.

"X Cantos," verse, *Michigan Quarterly Review,* 8, 1 (Winter 1969): 29-31.

1970   "Can There Be a National Policy for Stable Peace," *AAUW Journal,* 63, 4 (May 1970): 172-74. CP V, pp. 383-87.

"Dirge for an Urban Dweller," unpublished verse.

Economics as a Science (New York: McGraw-Hill, 1970).

"Fun and Games with the Gross National Product: The Role of Misleading Indicators in Social Policy," in *The Environmental Crisis: Man's Struggle to Live with Himself,* ed. Harold W. Helfrich, Jr. (New Haven: Yale University Press, 1970), pp. 157-70. CP III, pp. 467-82.

"Fundamental Considerations," in *Perspectives on Campus Tensions,* ed. David C. Nichols (Washington, D.C.: American Council on Education, 1970), pp. 3-17.

"A New Ethos for a New Era," in *Canada and the United States in the World of the Seventies,* ed. R. H. Wagenberg (Windsor, Ontario: University of Windsor Press, 1970), pp. 91-98.

A Primer on Social Dynamics: History as Dialectics and Development (New York: Free Press, 1970).

"The Real World of the Seventies and Beyond," in *Training a Ministry in the Seventies for a World of the Seventies and*

Beyond: 1969 Conference (New York: Association for Clinical Pastoral Education, 1970), pp. 10-22.

"Some Hesitant Reflections on the Political Future," in *1970 Coloradan,* Vol. 72 (Boulder: Associated Students of the University of Colorado, 1970), pp. 204-05.

"The War Industry and the American Economy," pamphlet, (De Kalb: Northern Illinois University Department of Economics, 1970). CP III, pp. 483-501.

1971   "Discussion" (of Allen V. Kneese, "Environmental Pollution: Economics and Policy"), *American Economic Review,* 61, 2 (May 1971): 167-69.

"Environment and Economics," in *Environment: Resources, Pollution & Society,* ed. William W. Murdoch (Stamford, Conn.: Sinauer Associates, 1971), pp. 359-67. CP III, pp. 569-79.

"The Ethics of Persuasion," unpublished paper.

"The Intellectual Framework of Bad Political Advice," review of W. W. Rostow, *Politics and the Stages of Growth, Virginia Quarterly Review,* 47, 4 (Autumn 1971): 602-07.

"Knowledge as a Road to Peace," *Bulletin of the Peace Studies Institute* (Manchester College, Ind.) (Aug. 1971): 1-4.

"The Meaning of Human Betterment," *Nebraska Journal of Economics and Business,* 10, 2 (Spring 1971): 3-12. CP IV, pp. 601-12.

"The Misallocation of Intellectual Resources in Economics," in *The Use and Abuse of Social Science,* ed. Irving L. Horowitz (New York: E. P. Dutton, for Transaction Books, 1971), pp. 34-51. CP III, pp. 533-52.

"The Need for Reform of National Income Statistics," in *Proceedings of the Social Statistics Section, 1970* (Washington, D.C.: American Statistical Association, 1971), pp. 94-97. CP III, pp. 581-86.

"Toward a Modest Society: The End of Growth and Grandeur," in *Economic Perspectives of Boulding and Samuelson* (Durham: Whittemore School of Business and Economics, University of New Hampshire, 1971), pp. 7-20; reply, pp. 21-22.

"What Do Economic Indicators Indicate?: Quality and Quantity in the GNP," in *The Economics of Pollution* (New York: New York University Press, 1971), pp. 31-80.

1972 "A Ballad of Ecological Awareness," verse, in *The Careless Technology: Ecology and International Development,* eds. M. Taghi Farvar and John P. Milton (Garden City, N. Y.: Natural History Press, for the Conservation Foundation and the Center for the Biology of Natural Systems, Washington University, 1972), pp. 3, 157, 371, 669, 793, 955.

"The Future of Personal Responsibility," *American Behavioral Scientist,* 15, 3 (Jan./Feb. 1972): 329-59. CP IV, pp. 535-67.

"The Household as Achilles' Heel," *Journal of Consumer Affairs,* 6, 2 (Winter 1972): 110-19.

"Human History in a Nutshell," unpublished verse.

"Introduction," in *Economic Imperialism: A Book of Readings,* eds. Kenneth Boulding and Tapan Mukerjee (Ann Arbor: University of Michigan Press, 1972), pp. ix-xviii.

"Man as a Commodity," in *Human Resources and Economic Welfare: Essays in Honor of Eli Ginzberg,* ed. Ivar Berg (New York: Columbia University Press, 1972), pp. 35-49. CP III, pp. 587-603.

"New Goals for Society?" in *Energy, Economic Growth, and the Environment,* ed. Sam H. Schurr (Baltimore: Johns Hopkins University Press, for Resources for the Future, 1972), pp. 139-51. CP IV, pp. 585-99.

"The Schooling Industry as a Possibly Pathological Section of the American Economy," *Review of Educational Research,* 42, 1 (Apr. 1972), 129-43. CP IV, pp. 569-84.

"Toward a Theory for the Study of Community," in *Issues in Community Organization,* ed. Lawrence Witmer (Chicago: Center for the Scientific Study of Religion, 1972), pp. 23-31.

"Towards a Twenty-First Century Politics," *Colorado Quarterly,* 20, 3 (Winter 1972): 309-19. CP V, pp. 407-19.

1973 "Aristocrats Have Always Been Sons of Bitches," *Psychology Today,* 6, 8 (Jan. 1973): 60-64, 67-68, 70, 86-87.

"Can There Be a Growth Policy?" in *Man and His Environment: The Vail Experience* (Vail, Colo.: The Printery, for the Town of Vail, 1973), p. 19.

The Economy of Love and Fear: A Preface to Grants Economics (Belmont, Calif.: Wadsworth, 1973).

"Foreword," in *Image and Environment: Cognitive Mapping and Spatial Behavior,* eds. Roger M. Downs and David Stea (Chicago: Aldine, 1973), pp. vii-ix.

"Foreword," in *The People: Growth and Survival,* Gerhard Hirschfeld (Chicago: Aldine, for the Council for the Study of Mankind, 1973), pp. xiii-xvi.

"General Systems as an Integrating Force in the Social Sciences," in *University Through Diversity: A Festschrift for Ludwig von Bertalanffy,* Vol. II, eds. William Gray and Nicholas D. Rizzo (New York: Gordon & Breach, 1973), pp. 951-67.

"Intersects: The Peculiar Organizations," in *Challenge to Leadership: Managing in a Changing World* (New York: Free Press, for the Conference Board, 1973), pp. 179-201.

"Looking Ahead. Interview: Kenneth E. Boulding," in *Economics '73-'74: Text* (Guilford, Conn.: Dushkin, 1973), pp. 10-11.

"Love, Fear, and the Economist," *Challenge,* 16, 3 (July-Aug. 1973), 32-39.

"Review of Richard A. Peterson, *The Industrial Order and Social Policy,*" *Administrative Science Quarterly,* 18, 4 (Dec. 1973), 555-56.

1974   "Bottleneck Economics," *Technology Review,* 76, 6 (May 1974): 16-17.

"Defense Against Unwanted Change," lecture, Massachusetts Institute of Technology.

"Foreword," in *Creative Tension: The Life and Thought of Kenneth Boulding,* Cynthia Kerman (Ann Arbor: University of Michigan Press, 1974), pp. v-vii.

"Love," unpublished verse.

"Minus the Spark," review of John Kenneth Galbraith,

Economics & the Public Purpose, Monthly Labor Review, 97, 10 (Oct. 1974): 80-81.

"The Quality of Life and Economic Affluence," in *Environmental Spectrum: Social and Economic Views on the Quality of Life,* eds. Ronald O. Clarke and Peter List (New York: D. Van Nostrand, 1974), pp. 82-95.

"Reflections on Planning: The Value of Uncertainty," *Technology Review,* 77, 1 (Oct./Nov. 1974): 8.

"The Social System and the Energy Crisis," *Science,* 184, 4134 (Apr. 19, 1974): 255-57.

"What Went Wrong, If Anything, Since Copernicus?," *Bulletin of the Atomic Scientists,* 30, 1 (Jan. 1974): 17-23; also available on tape in the "Speaking of Science," Conversations With Outstanding Scientists series, Vol. III. (Washington, D.C.: American Association for the Advancement of Science, 1973).

"The World as an Economic Region," in *Regional Economic Policy: Proceedings of a Conference* (Minneapolis: Federal Reserve Bank of Minneapolis, June 1974), pp. 27-34.

1975   "The Clouded Future of the American Economy: Implications for Older Consumers," in *Proceedings of the National Forum on Consumer Concerns of Older Americans, Washington, D.C., June 1-3, 1975* (Washington, D.C.: National Retired Teachers Association/American Association of Retired Persons, 1975), pp. 13-31; discussion, 31-35.

"Dialogue: Civilized Society," with John Kenneth Galbraith, *The Mainichi Daily News* (English edition) and *The Mainichi Shimbun* (Japanese edition), serialized beginning Oct. 14, 1975; ending Dec. 27, 1965 (61 segments).
"Doers and Stoppers," *Technology Review,* 78, 1(Oct./Nov. 1975): 8.

"Entropy Economics," in *Public Utility Regulation: Change and Scope,* eds. Werner Sichel and Thomas G. Gies (Lexington, Mass.: Lexington Books/D.C. Heath, 1975), pp. 1-12.

"The International System in the Eighties: Models of International Peace," in *Dynamics of a Conflict: A Reexamination of the Arab-Israeli Conflict,* ed. Gabriel Sheffer (Atlantic Highlands, N. J.: Humanities Press, for the Van Leer Jerusalem Foundation, 1975), pp. 3-18.

"Justifications for Inequality: The Contributions of Economic Theory," (Cambridge, Mass.: MIT Technology and Culture Seminar, 1975).

"Mitosis (The Amoeba Speaks)," unpublished verse.

"Verses from the National Institute of Education Meeting," unpublished.

1976 "Colorado's Kenneth Boulding: A World Renowned Scholar Forecasts Our Future," *Denver Magazine* (July 1976): 47-49, 71-72.

"Energy and the Environment," (Laramie: College of Commerce and Industry, University of Wyoming, Jan. 1976); occasional paper # 1.

"Foreword," in *Communicating Across Cultures For What?* eds. John C. Condon and Mitsuko Saito (Tokyo: Simul Press, 1976), pp. i-iii.

"Inflation and the Social Contract," *Technology Review,* 78, 3 (Jan. 1976): 3.

"Isaac Watts Revised," verse, in *Finite Resources and the Human Future,* ed. Ian G. Barbour (Minneapolis: Augsburg Publishing House, 1976), pp. 155-67.

"The Next 200 Years," in *Finite Resources and the Human Future,* ed. Ian G. Barbour, (Minneapolis: Augsburg Publishing House, 1976), pp. 155-67.

"Notes From Woods Hole," unpublished verse.

"Outrageous Fortune," *Technology Review,* 79, 1 (Oct./ Nov. 1976): 4-5.

"Scholarly Rights and Political Morality," in *Controversies and Decisions: The Social Sciences and Public Policy,* ed. Charles Frankel (New York: Russell Sage Foundation, for the American Academy of Arts and Sciences Project on

Social Science Controversies and Public Policy Decisions, 1976), pp. 205-17.

"Toward a Theory of Discrimination," in *Equal Employment Opportunity and the A.T. & T. Case,* ed. Phyllis A. Wallace (Cambridge, Mass.: MIT Press, 1976), pp. 9-15.

Index

The Bouldingisms and General Subject Index

Printed in the United States
by Baker & Taylor Publisher Services